The
Mercy
Seat

God at work in a GP's surgery

Gill Cronau

malcolm down
PUBLISHING

25 24 23 22   7 6 5 4 3 2 1

First published 2022 by Malcolm Down Publishing Ltd.
www.malcolmdown.co.uk
Registered Office: Welwyn Garden City, England

British Library Cataloguing in Publication Data
A catalogue record for this book is available from the British Library.

ISBN 978-1-915046-19-2

Cover design by Robin Ireland, Pepperfish.co.uk

Art direction by Sarah Grace

Printed in the UK

What Others Are Saying About *The Mercy Seat*...

In *The Mercy Seat*, you will find page after page of faith-filled and utterly inspirational stories that will create in you hunger to see Jesus move in your workplace, family and everyday lives. Gill's powerful authenticity and courage shine all the way through this book and I utterly commend it to you in the hope that it will provoke you to a life of prophetic kindness towards people whom he loves. God's mercies are new every morning and this book underlines that truth in a most profound way.

Phil Wilthew
Author of *Developing Prophetic Culture and Multiplying Disciples*

When I first became a Christian, I had no idea that I was called to do the stuff that Jesus did; that my mandate was to proclaim and demonstrate His kingdom wherever I go. Over the years I have been on a journey of learning what it looks like to follow Jesus really closely.

Every so often I meet people who have really caught this same vision. People who live with a deep-rooted conviction that their mandate is to bring God's kingdom in their place of influence. Their passion to reveal Jesus motivates them to keep being obedient to Him, even when it's costly and they risk being misunderstood. These people have seen something of Jesus and His kingdom that means they can never be the same again. Their life is no longer their own, they have been bought with a high price. The only appropriate response to Jesus' amazing grace is to gladly surrender to Him.

Gill is one of these heroes of the faith. She is one of the most inspiring people I know when it comes to seeing God's kingdom come in her workplace. I have seen her journey first-hand as she has pursued a naturally supernatural life, through the ups and the downs. Her courage to keep saying yes to Jesus is unique and beautiful and her faith and passion to see more of His kingdom is infectious. It constantly amazes me that, in the midst of what can often be a hard and discouraging environment, she sees life and hope flow. She always has stories of God breaking in and I cannot wait for you to read some of them in this book.

If you work in the healthcare sector, I know that this book is going to give you hope and faith for more. My prayer is that you will receive an impartation from the Holy Spirit as you read Gill's stories, so that her ceiling in God would become your floor. God wants you to partner with Him so that many, many people in your care encounter His love and kindness. This is what you've been made for!

If, like me, your area of influence is different to Gill's, let her stories inspire you and stir your faith for the people and places you're called to impact. All of us are invited into a life-giving adventure of proclaiming and demonstrating God's kingdom wherever we have influence. The truth is that God wants to use ordinary people like you and me to change the world, one encounter at a time. I want to encourage you to pray that your heart and mind would wake up to this truth as you read this book. God has prepared so many good works for us to step into. Let's not settle for anything less.

Without God we can do nothing. With God anything is possible!

Wendy Mann
Wendy Mann Equip
Author of *Naturally Supernatural* and *Leading as Sons and Daughters*

Gill is a woman of faith, hungry and willing to take risks to see God's kingdom come, and someone who regularly sees the power of God's love bringing healing and transformation.

I have the privilege of knowing Gill as a friend and whenever I hear stories of what she has seen God do, I come away inspired by her childlike faith and simple obedience to the promptings of the Holy Spirit.

Moved with compassion, Gill is willing to push past fear to love the one in front of her. She daily looks for opportunities to partner with the one who she knows is completely kind and full of mercy, inviting people to know him.

It is my pleasure to recommend this book to you. Reading these stories, I was deeply moved by God's love and compassion for those who are hurting and broken, and I was reminded afresh how they represent the Father's heart of love for each one of us.

Jesus said when you pray, pray that his kingdom would come on earth, as it is in heaven. I encourage you to read this book and, whatever your sphere of influence is, to allow these stories to release faith in you for what is possible as you partner with the King of heaven.

Claire Coggan
Author of *Go: Everyday Stories of Stopping to Love*

Contents

Acknowledgements

This book is all about the mercy of Jesus, his healing hands and his huge heart of redeeming love. It is not a book containing teaching, it is not meant to be a bible study or to instruct; rather it is a collection of testimonies, gathered over a period of time. My hope in writing it is to inspire people towards faith and courage, to help them see what is possible with God, particularly those working in the field of healthcare and psychological wellbeing services.

Many people have inspired me on my own journey in this respect, too many to number here, but I would especially like to acknowledge my church leaders at the King's Arms Church who have seen and understood the value of people's contribution to the kingdom of heaven in their workplaces, and have championed and resourced them to succeed.

I am so grateful to Wendy Mann for her pioneering spirit and for first giving me a 'platform' to share a miraculous testimony from my place of work, and to all my friends, especially Marco, who inspired and encouraged me within the King's Arms School of Supernatural Ministry to take risks, grow in the prophetic gifts, and to be accountable.

I am grateful to my dear friend Claire for being a great mentor, encourager and partner in the gospel, and for Sarah who never fails to shower love and encouragement on me. I am grateful to people I have never met, whose laid-down lives of radical love and faith have challenged me and called me out of my personal comfort zone, and to worship leaders worldwide who have sung songs that took me deeper, to where the love of Jesus overwhelmed me to the point I could not stay in the shallows.

I am grateful to Dr Pete Carter and all the other courageous people who have pioneered 'Heaven in Healthcare', a movement and network of healthcare professionals seeking heaven's solutions for the NHS. Every

Heaven in Healthcare conference I have attended has helped to increase my boldness and faith that anything is possible with God.

I am so grateful for the friends who told me I should write a book, and then encouraged me on the journey of attempting to do something I have never done before.

I would also like to thank the amazing Jane Sanders for editing my script and giving me her invaluable perspective. I could not have come this far on my journey without her help.

I am grateful to Steve, my husband, who has such a tender heart towards Jesus, and carries such a revelation of the Father heart of God. He has been my greatest listener and support, especially on the days when things haven't gone so well in the work place.

Mostly I am thankful to my best friend the Holy Spirit for his constant pursuit of me, for always being available, and for showing up when I need him most.

Foreword

Gill Cronau and I have known each other since we were junior doctors. We first met each other whilst we were both training to become General Practitioners (GPs) and the context of that specific meeting was a Christian gathering in which we were discussing how Christian faith could stand alongside medicine in a way that was suitable, contemporary and helpful.

Both of us have always been fully convinced that our Christianity gives us spiritual resources that can enhance the standard of medicine that we practice and we have sought to lead naturally supernatural lifestyles to make those resources available to other people. Over the years we have shared stories of God's intervention in the lives of our patients, colleagues and also in our own lives. We have seen God do amazing things.

I am so grateful to know Gill who continues to inspire and encourage me, I have learned many things from her as have many others including participants in 'Heaven in Healthcare'. Two things stand out to me about Gill: her compassion for people and her trust in God.

In this book, *The Mercy Seat*, she relates real-life stories that illustrate those two attributes in beautiful ways that will stir your heart and inspire your mind. These are very real stories that illustrate the love of God towards humanity and his willingness to intervene in people's lives through his family on earth, his sons and daughters.

I found myself turning page after page eager to read the next installment of an amazing overarching story, the story of a daughter of God reaching out to others through her medical practice, not only practicing great medicine but also demonstrating the love and power of God.

I found the very practical advice at the end of the book extremely helpful and it will probably answer questions that may arise in your mind as you read.

I am convinced this book will also enrich your life as you read it.

Thank you, Gill; once again you have inspired and encouraged me, and thank you Jesus who sacrificed his everything to enable the love and power of God to be experienced on planet Earth.

Dr Pete Carter MBChB

Founder of Heaven in Healthcare www.heaveninhealthcare.com

Author of *Faith - discovering and using the resources of heaven* and *Unwrapping Lazarus*

Director of Eastgate church www.eastgate.org.uk

The Meaning Behind the Title

I remember a long time ago, Gill and I and another friend had a time of prayer together in our home, about our places of work. When it came to praying for Gill, I had this picture of angels in her office, covering her room, particularly standing over the chair where her patients sit when they come to see her in their time of need. I could see that the angels were covering that chair with their wings, and it was as if Gill's office had become like a type of Holy of Holies. That chair was a special place and angels were covering it.

It seemed to me that the purpose of them being there was to protect the person as they sat and began to engage in their consultation: to protect them from all the garbage that the enemy had been dumping into their minds and hearts, including confusion, destructive lies and condemnation. Protected in this way, patients could sit and meet with God, and hear God speak through whatever insight or wisdom or word of knowledge or prophetic word Gill had for them. The angels were creating this prepared, sanctified holy place where God could really speak and connect with people.

Then it occurred to me that this is actually a picture of the Mercy Seat described in Exodus 25, where we read that God explained to Moses how to create the atonement cover over the Ark of the Covenant, with the angels extending their wings over it. Exodus 25:20-22 says the angels' wings are to overshadow the cover, and that God will speak to Moses there. Exodus 33:11 confirms how God indeed spoke to Moses 'face to face, as a man speaks with his friend'.

The purpose of the atonement cover, it seems, was to provide a place where God could meet with and speak to his people. But because of their imperfection and fearful response to his invitation they were unable to come close, and so the designated meeting place, where the presence of God manifested, had to be separated from them by a

13

curtain. Only Moses could come into the presence and speak to God. But many centuries later, when Jesus died, the curtain was ripped in two, symbolising that there was now an open invitation for all people to come into the presence of God.

That's what happens in Gill's office. It's a place where heaven meets earth. God literally overshadows and speaks to people when they are in that chair.

Hebrews 4:16 says, in the Passion translation:

'So now we come freely and boldly to the place where love is enthroned and receive mercy's kiss, and discover the grace we urgently need to strengthen us in our time of weakness.' (TPT)

Steve Cronau

Author's Note

The stories in this book contain many examples of prophetic gifting being used in various ways. Prophecy is one of the gifts of the Holy Spirit, and one that the apostle Paul particularly encourages us to pursue. 1 Corinthians 14:1 and 3 says, 'Follow the way of love, and eagerly desire gifts of the Spirit, especially prophecy' and 'The one who prophesies speaks to people for their strengthening, encouragement and comfort.'

The gift of prophecy as taught in the New Testament is, at its simplest, a message of encouragement or comfort for a particular person or group of people in a particular moment and situation, and it will never contradict or add to what is already revealed in the Bible.

I believe that God is always wanting to communicate with people and show his deep love for them, and that one of the ways he does this is through the prophetic. As we seek to bless, encourage and help people, we can look to him first to reveal to us something of his thoughts and feelings about a person, and then to show us how to communicate those thoughts and feelings in a way the person can understand and relate to.

1 Corinthians 14:1 tells us that the prophetic gift is not unobtainable or only for a very few people, but that each one of us can pursue and operate in this wonderful gift, which is so powerful for helping other people to encounter the goodness and kindness of God.

The following stories give some examples of what that can look like in everyday life. Please understand as you read them that they are occurring within the context of providing excellent general medical care in an ordinary GP practice. I would also like to reassure the readers that they are all patient led consultations, and where names have been given, they have been changed to honour their privacy. In every case where possible, permissions from the patients were sought and granted to allow their stories to be told in a book form. Many expressed delight that their stories of what they had been through might be helpful to others in the course of time.

Chapter 1 – God's Repair Shop

'The heart of generosity brings people to God ...The more than enough that God blesses us with, is not to build our kingdoms or empires, but to extravagantly bless those around us.'
Bill Johnson

She sat down in the patient's chair and began to explain her predicament. She was distraught with defeat, full of tears, and there were tangible waves of personal disappointment and shame in the atmosphere. This young woman was someone I was well acquainted with, and who I knew had struggled for many years with a powerful cocaine addiction. She admitted she had been in a downward spiral lately, due to her relinquishing control to the drug, resulting in unpaid bills, debt, and real peril with the risk of the bailiffs coming to remove her possessions.

A couple of years previous to this, she had disclosed her drug addiction to me, after years of covering it up. I became the first person to know that she had spent her inheritance from her father on the drug, a huge sum of several thousand pounds, and was now without resource.

She had experienced a tremendous number of heavy losses in her young life: her beloved father who had given her a sense of worth and safety, several unborn children lost through miscarriages and a stillbirth, and many turbulent relationships with men that had left her feeling worthless. She also shared with me on one occasion her lack of self-esteem and her revulsion at her appearance. She felt she lacked features typical of classic femininity, and told me she 'did not feel like a proper woman'.

I remember on that occasion a strong and clear instruction from the Holy Spirit about what I needed to do: I was to give her a threefold gift, upon her attending her follow-up appointment. I was to give her pink lilies to look at and smell, a card with a message from the Father for her to read and a worship song for her to listen to. The Father wanted to overwhelm her senses and communicate the extent of his love and commitment to her. She wept during the song, such tears I can never forget. She was in the Mercy Seat and God was very close.

And now here she was again, with a beautiful sense that the room was prepared as she sat down, and I was ready to speak some insights into her life regarding the addiction. I explained how the substance becomes something the addict develops a relationship with, that eventually replaces all other relationships; how It becomes that 'go to' place for numbing out.

This time she was ready, she said, for the part of her that was drawn to addiction to 'die' and for her true self to 'come back to life'. I told her it was like a seed falling into the ground and being buried, then a new plant coming up and eventually becoming a sheaf of wheat and producing something really beautiful that can nourish others (John 12:24). I explained the meaning of 'redemption', gave her a small fragment of pottery, with the word 'Redeemed' written on it, and explained the good news of the gospel, the whole journey of Jesus coming from heaven to redeem what was broken and lost and far away. We agreed that it was time for her to let go of her old life as an addict. I prayed for her to be released from addiction, for her true self to come to the fore, and that Jesus would help her live this new life.

She got up quite tearfully, saying she felt a little wobbly and strange; it was a precious moment, as the Lord intervened and encountered someone at their most vulnerable, when nobody else could.

She phoned me recently, not with a medical problem, but to tell me she has begun to engage with youths in her area, and look after them like a mother. She wants to mentor them in what she has learned about the danger of drugs and of making poor choices in their already troubled lives. I was able to speak prophetically over her and encourage her that she was now becoming a mother, that God was giving her lots of children to care for, and that she needed to keep learning about him, so as to keep passing on to others what she was learning. I do not know whether she has become a follower of Jesus yet, but she is on the journey, and already has a wonderful story to tell of how God met with her and changed her life.

I find myself overwhelmed by the beauty of this woman's story from its beginning to the present. It stands as a reminder that every life matters, no matter how broken and misguided, and every life in the Mercy Seat can be transformed by love.

When we look at people in this way, not focusing solely on all the problems and the flawed nature of humanity, but instead seeing people the way God sees them, and catching a glimpse of the future destiny he has for them, it transforms our work as healthcare professionals from an experience of toil and frustration which can lead to exhaustion and a measure of hopelessness, into a joyful work of restoration.

One of my current favourite TV shows is BBC's *The Repair Shop*. I love the way each craftsperson, uniquely experienced in their field, receives an object and begins to absorb the story of the person who is entrusting it to them for repair. They have a vision of how the person's face will light up when they see the fully restored object, because they have listened first to the history and emotions connected with the object. That energises them for all the painstaking, intricate repair work, which just blows my mind – would I have such patience and perseverance? But this is so like the nature of the Father – to repair all the dents and breakages, replace long-lost missing bits, clean clogged up mechanisms and restore the colour and texture that give each piece its unique character and beauty. It's a good picture of the work of the kingdom, work in which we have the privilege of partnering with the Father.

I believe that thinking this way starts when we first allow him to come and work in our own lives... the journey into knowing the Father's heart for us. This has been my journey over many years, and one that I know I'll never fully get to the end of this side of eternity, because he's just that good a Father! But I know that every day, if I see another person the way he does, I'll understand yet another facet of his love and mercy.

Chapter 2 – Blessed are the Peacemakers

'Blessed are the peacemakers, for they will be called children of God.'
Jesus (Matthew 5:9)

'If you wash the feet of another person, you find out why they walk the way they do.'
Heidi Baker

There was a big altercation at the door of the surgery. Someone was trying to get in to see a doctor, but was unwilling to wear a mask. This was the season during the Covid-19 pandemic when no one was allowed into the surgery without a prior appointment and a face covering. The receptionist was refusing point blank to let him into the building, and tensions were rising. Another younger and less experienced trainee receptionist came over and tried to resolve the situation, but only made it worse. He had a loud, deep voice, and probably came across as quite intimidating. Voices rose, insults began to fly, the young receptionist called him something that should never be said to a patient, and he became even more upset and angry! Then another colleague arrived on the scene and dismissed him firmly without further discussion.

He went home, but was soon on the phone to the practice manager, asking for a meeting to discuss the incident, and threatening legal action against the practice because of the way he had been treated. It was a mess, a no-win situation. The patient was unhappy, the young receptionist was facing dismissal, and the practice was facing the unwelcome prospect of legal action. The news of all this came to my ears that lunchtime. I knew the man well – I had looked after him for at least ten years and knew that he had suffered a number of serious and life-threatening medical problems – and I felt immediately prompted by the Holy Spirit to ask him for his solution.

Ten years earlier, this man had been a long-standing alcoholic, who couldn't break free from a lifestyle that revolved around heavy consumption of cider and spirits. But after a few months of consulting with him, we developed a good rapport. I would listen and often pray for him, and there came a point when I said I would pray for him to break free from the addiction if he would make a decision to reduce his drinking. I remember feeling there was a kind of transaction between me and God after I finished praying for him. That night, he later told me, he had an experience where he felt suddenly empowered, and from that moment on didn't want to drink any more – he just stopped instantly and has never drunk since! It was amazing to me, as alcohol is the hardest addictive substance to just suddenly stop. He was quite a new man, beginning to stay awake by day, and to sleep better at night, when he had previously been almost nocturnal. He took up martial arts as a sport to improve his health, he was eating healthily, losing weight and spending time with his daughter at weekends. God was absolutely involved with this miracle and the man absolutely knew it – he always allowed me to pray with him when he came for a consultation in the years that followed.

But here was this mess that we were all in, and I knew that the Father had other plans.

I telephoned the man and arranged for him to come in and see me the next day to address his medical needs. That evening, I went for a prayer walk to pray about him and other matters. As I walked under a horse chestnut tree I spotted a beautiful shiny conker, which immediately made me think about my childhood and the conker games I used to love to play at school with my friends. As I picked the conker up, I sensed the Holy Spirit speaking to me, giving me a message of hope for this man's future, and a message of how God knew all about his past right from his childhood, the early years of repeated foster care placements, the losses of his youth, his innocence, his safety, his father's protection, the loss of the years of his twenties and thirties through addiction, the loss of his health through recent illnesses and the onset of arthritis, and now his loss of dignity and reputation at the door of the one institution that he was looking to for help. I sensed the Holy Spirit saying that I was to put the man's name on that conker, give it to him with the prophetic message, and share with him the Father's deep knowledge and love for him.

So when he arrived at his appointment, the Mercy Seat was ready and available for him and we began to unpack all the recent events in a calm, gentle manner. We started with the medical problems, putting them all into perspective and addressing his worst fears. Then I apologised for the receptionist's words and behaviour, explained the situation, and began to tell him the story of how I found the conker, and the message Father God had for him.

He agreed with me about the story of his life losses, amazed that God had seen him through all the years of loss, and known him for who he really is. I was able to speak the Father's opinion of him, his loving compassionate heart towards him, and then I spoke to him about his future, how there could now be a new starting point with an end to the cycle of loss, and the beginning of gain, starting with his dignity and reputation being restored. I placed my hand on his and prayed for him, and gave him his conker – which he loved and promised to keep. As I finished praying, he exclaimed, 'No one has touched me in 6 months!' It was a precious moment that I will never forget – the kindness of the Father and the redemptive purposes he has for every situation.

There was no further trouble between this man and the surgery after that.

♡ ♡

This story illustrates the kindness of the Father, how he knows the shoes we walk in and why we walk the way we do. I love how this connects with us being peacemakers, as we give grace to people, knowing we have never been in their situation, and could not know how we would respond under the same pressure and duress, had we had the same upbringing and life experiences. It's our mandate and privilege to be peacemakers.

The story also illustrates how we can use prophetic gifts to help bring about God's desired outcome. In this case, I used a physical object to communicate a meaning which the person was well able to understand and identify with.

And I love the way in which the Father loves to speak to us if our hearts are willing to obey him no matter how unusual the instruction will be. If our 'yes' is already sealed, it attracts heaven to show us more. It was a risk, I'll admit to that, and even now it sounds improbable that this could happen during a consultation at a doctor's surgery! This is what I call the 'tenth door'. When, metaphorically speaking, nine doors are shut due to fear, politics, offence, cultural barriers etc, the Holy Spirit knows how to open a tenth door and connect with a person he loves. It's the 'soft place', like a unique bespoke key to unlock a person's heart. The way he does this never fails to amaze me. His presence is able to flow under the threshold of the door, to change even seemingly impossible situations.

We just need to ask, and these prophetic keys will be given to us. It's his pleasure to colour outside the lines of what seems possible.

Chapter 3 – The Power of Blessing

'The tongue has the power of life and death.'
Proverbs 18:21

'The Lord bless you and keep you; the Lord make his face shine upon you and be gracious to you; the Lord turn his face towards you and give you peace.'
Numbers 6:24-26

I was sitting at my desk early one morning, and decided to begin my working day by listening to an audio testimony forwarded to me via WhatsApp and entitled 'The power of blessing'.

It was the story of a gynaecologist in the USA who heard from the Holy Spirit that she was to openly pray for and bless all the members of her team in the operating theatre before her patients went under anaesthetic for their operations. She reported that this often led to much better outcomes from surgery, and that on the first occasion she introduced this initiative, almost everyone seemed moved to the point of tears and felt greatly empowered. It was such a stunning act of faith, with the result that God seemed to honour her and give better outcomes than would naturally be expected. Furthermore, one unbelieving member of the team witnessed a miracle one day when a new-born infant was revived after a stillbirth; he later gave his life to Jesus, having realised the power and presence of God in those sessions!

As I listened I thought to myself, 'Shall I ask for this today?' And of course, the Holy Spirit said, 'By all means. I want to do that again with you today.'

Later that morning a lady brought her five-year-old son to see me, very worried about his separation anxiety, school refusal, and new onset of fearfulness and insecurity. As she described all this, I wondered what lay behind this change in the child's behaviour. I asked her if there had been an event preceding this, and she replied yes, he had been frightened one day on the path to school by a very disturbed local man with mental health issues, who had shouted at them and intimidated them both.

I was concerned that this whole family seemed to be afflicted with anxiety of various degrees, including the child's mum, and two older sisters. As I looked at the child's gorgeous little face, I felt an enormous affection for him, and something akin to Holy Spirit defiance rose up in me – 'No! Not this one as well...!'

His mum had been very kind and generous to us at the surgery during the pandemic and had collected items from her community to make care packages for us all, a wonderful act of extreme generosity welling up from her own extreme poverty.

As she was leaving the room, I told her, 'I have something for you.'

She said, 'You don't need to give us anything.' She was thinking about material gifts, which is her way of serving the community.

'No,' I said, 'This isn't something I paid for, it's a blessing. I want to ask you to allow me to pray a prayer of blessing over the two of you. I could do it after you leave here, but I believe if you hear it, faith will rise up in you and it will have more impact.'

She readily agreed and I began to pray and declare blessing, not knowing what would come out of my mouth. I started with the little boy, how amazing he was, how much he was loved and liked at school and how much he would be missed if he wasn't there. I declared prophetically over his life that he was to be confident, happy and full of joy, and know how important and special he is. Then I spoke over his mum, thanking Jesus for her amazing gift of generosity and her fierce love for her children. I spoke health and mental wellbeing over them both, then they left the consultation room and went home.

During the course of the following week, the mum rang up for a prescription for herself, and told me 'That prayer of yours worked a treat. He went to school just fine on Monday and every day since!'

I was literally dancing in my room. How good of God to show up like that! There really is power in a blessing when given with faith and compassion.

During the Covid-19 pandemic, there was little opportunity for face-to-face consulting, and nearly all of our work was over the phone. There was so much fear of the unknown for all of us, including our patients. I took the opportunity to say 'Bless you,' as I said goodbye at the end of a call, and sometimes I would feel the prompting of Holy Spirit to pray or prophesy over a patient. One lady, who is a nurse at our local hospital, and actually contracted Covid through her work, was at home, breathless and unwell, with five children and her husband to look after. I was able to have a video call with her, and seeing her situation I became overwhelmed with concern and compassion for her, isolated and sick with her large family depending on her. So I summoned up my courage and I asked if she would let me pray a blessing over her and her whole family, which she readily did. She told me she was a believer.

Months later, I received a beautiful thank-you card, telling me how she had recovered completely, beginning shortly after that prayer, and that none of her family had become sick. She had been able to return to work and was back on the wards. She was so grateful that her doctor would do that for her. I have since had the opportunity to pray for her daughter too, who remembered well her mother's miracle blessing.

I am in awe of our Father's blessing and it has taught me so much about the power of our words. Now I am more aware than ever of the importance of managing my words, so that a blessing is embedded in everything I say. I try to help people adjust the way they talk about themselves, too.

Chapter 4 – 'Just Give Me Something to Work With'

'Royalty is my identity, servant hood is my assignment, intimacy
with God is my life source ...Before people I am a servant, before
God I am an intimate son or daughter, before the powers of hell I
am a ruler, with zero tolerance for its influence.'
Bill Johnson

I like to ask the Holy Spirit for creative ways of helping people access
the healing Father heart of God, but some people are just so broken, so
damaged, that it seems overwhelmingly difficult to help them.

But one day an idea came to me to prepare some pieces of broken tile
and pottery, with significant redemptive words on them for people to
connect with. People are very open to symbolism, and one word given
in this way can trigger a whole conversation or change of heart that
would not happen through a natural conversation. It's one of the ways
I engage with prophecy in the context of helping people connect to the
Father and relate to his opinion of them, or a truth about themselves, or
something he wants them to access in the realm of healing.

On one occasion I was with a lady who came into see me very low
in mood, actually feeling heartbroken, exactly one year on from the
unfortunate death of her daughter, who had been only in her twenties.
The daughter had been unwell for years with serious illnesses affecting
her bowel and kidneys, and was extremely vulnerable. Unfortunately, she
had been taken advantage of by her so-called 'carer', a much older man,
who used her benefits money and sold off many of her pain medications
for profit. The mother had suspected this terrible exploitation, but was
never able to prove it and had always felt helpless to intervene. She
had lost her husband to cancer years before, and her other daughter's

partner had died through a deliberate overdose. And now she had lost her daughter as well.

That day she told me she hated her daughter's carer, with everything in her being and could never forgive him, but at the same time she asked me to help her out of this dark place. I remember her tears and the strain on her face from carrying all this toxic emotion, which had taken its toll on her mental and physical wellbeing.

I thought of my pottery pieces and had a lightning nudge from Holy Spirit to show her all of them by spreading them out on my desk, and asking her which one she would like to pick out. She picked 'Freedom'.

I knew then that we would have to talk about forgiveness. I explained that the only way out for her, to gain her own freedom, was to forgive. She looked horrified at the thought; forgiveness seemed impossible to her. So I explained simply and clearly what forgiveness actually is: that is, relinquishing the right to be judge, and allowing God his rightful place to be the just judge, thereby allowing us to release the person and the offence. We prayed, and in that moment, the Holy Spirit was present to enable her to hand over the pain and the offence to Jesus. In that place of vulnerability, Jesus came and began to heal her heart, as I continued to pray and relate her situation to his suffering and humiliation on the cross for her, and for everyone else including the man she hated. It was a beautiful moment right there in the midst of a busy morning surgery.

She got up to go home and took the pottery piece, which I wrapped in tissue paper for her, and with tears in her eyes, she hugged me. The next day I received a message from her: 'Thank you for my freedom.'

This lady is one of those precious people with a simple, childlike faith, with nothing complicated or sophisticated in her nature, and is wonderfully open to the tender love of God. I often pass some worship songs on to her, and she listens to them and tells me how she encounters God's presence right there in her home. When she comes to see me for a consultation, she never comes empty-handed, but brings a small gift of flowers or something she has made. I find this gratitude and generosity overflowing from her poverty quite overwhelming. I know her name is known in heaven, where her love and patient endurance will be rewarded one day, and her compensation will be complete.

♡ ♡

The desire for connection is so strong in the heart of God, that he rushes in when we reach out to him. He literally says to us, 'Just give me something to work with and I'll do the rest.'

I have given these shards of tile, usually black with gold words painted on them, to countless people. The words I paint on them are redemptive, such as: safe, peace, loved, healed, seen, known, valuable, precious, cherished etc. I had one piece – actually from a flowerpot, so it was really rough and untidy – with 'PRINCESS' written on it in gold paint. The lady who received this was a breast cancer patient, only thirty-three years old, a single mother with three young children. Her cancer treatment had caused her weight gain, hair loss and disfigured body shape following her mastectomy. She was crying in the nurse's treatment room after having her hormone injection, which is given to block the effects of oestrogen on the tumour and so prevent the cancer spreading. The nurse called me in to help, as the woman was inconsolable and almost hysterical.

I saw her then with the Father's eyes, and was filled with compassion. She was wearing a bobble hat to conceal her thinning hair, and a big, baggy overcoat to disguise her body shape. I felt that she was full of shame and self-hatred, trapped in this changed body that was now hers, and I knew that her physical appearance was something she had always taken pleasure in. I ran back to my room and collected the 'Princess' piece, then on my knees I presented it to her and explained its symbolism. I told her she was a *princess*, that she might not feel like it, or look like one on the outside, but that was how God saw her and it was her true identity.

Two weeks later, that same nurse saw her again and reported to me that the woman was now back at work, the woolly hat was off, she was in a nice dress, and much brighter and in a much better frame of mind. The woman herself has told me since that she keeps the 'Princess' piece on her dressing table and looks at it every day. We have linked her with a health coach for ongoing support on her difficult journey ahead, and I pray for her often in my personal time, for healing of her mind and body, and that she might know the one who wants to give her a new identity.

I have another patient who told me he carries his 'hope' piece in his pocket all the time, and has recently come out of a dark depression and profound hopelessness.

It's just a 'piece' of the story of their recovery, but it matters. It symbolises the kindness, mercy and healing that come from God, and brings together the whole of their healing journey, including medicine and surgery. The redemptive words can give hope to hold onto in a seemingly hopeless situation, and can speak of a different future reality from the one the person is currently experiencing.

Chapter 5 – Stop for the One

One of the greatest influencers in my life is without a doubt Heidi Baker, and this one simple phrase of hers, 'Stop for the one', has totally changed my way of working. In a work environment that is pressured, busy, full-on and, quite frankly, rushed, love looks like slowing down, and if possible stopping, for that one person that God has clearly seen, fully known and brought to me with loving kindness. I have made it my goal to intentionally look for that person and when I do, the Holy Spirit always does something that causes my heart to rejoice.

I remember how one Friday lunchtime I had shut down my computer, packed up my things and was heading out of the door of my room, when I had this thought: 'I didn't 'stop' for that one person today.' I said to the Father, 'I'm so sorry – I just didn't see anyone in that way today, please forgive me'. I walked out of the corridor into the waiting room, and there was one patient sitting there, waiting to see one of my colleagues.

I noted his body posture. He was cupping his head in his hands, and rocking back and forth, groaning. He looked dishevelled and thin. I stopped and asked him, 'Are you ok?' I knew he was going to be seen by someone else, but I sensed the Holy Spirit was with me in that moment with him. He told me about the headaches, the stress he was going through, his frustration and desperation in getting some help, his sense of feeling judged and stigmatised over his request for pain medication. There had been a breakdown of trust between him and the healthcare professionals, so he was only allowed two or three days' medication at a time, which meant he had to continually keep asking but often felt he couldn't, so he would wait until he was desperate.

'Come and see me on Monday, and I will help you,' was what came out of my mouth. I prayed for him all weekend, hoping he would call... and sure enough, he was on my call-back list on Monday morning. An hour later he was sitting in the Mercy Seat.

He suffered from migraine, that was clear, but there was so much more going on besides. He had been an addict and had spent time in prison for drug offences. He had been homeless, but was now living in a hostel with his son who he doted on. He was finding it hard raising a teenager in this environment. He mentioned the noise, the chaos, the lack of privacy, the fear of violence and theft, and the disruption to his son's schooling. It really was a desperate situation, and it seemed that the headaches were just the outcome of years of attrition and the struggle for survival.

I listened and spoke kindly to him, conscious of the importance of giving him a voice and dignity, and of believing his story. It is very costly for people with trauma when they are not believed, but believing them costs me nothing. I told him about the Father's love, prayed for his headaches, gave him some migraine prevention treatment, and arranged a follow-up appointment for the next week. He came to the follow-up with a smile on his face. He had had no more headaches, and was keen to tell me more of his story.

Years ago, he had become a believer while he was in prison in Bedford. Once released, he was contacted on the streets by an outreach team from the King's Arms Project, who offered him support and housing, and eventually he was baptised in King's Arms Church. After some time he unfortunately got back into drugs, fell away from the Christian community in Bedford and ended up in Peterborough, where his son was born, and was now trying very hard to grapple his way back into mainstream living.

I was able this time to unpack more of the Father heart of God, telling him, 'You never stop being a son or a daughter. Once adopted, we will always belong in God's family.' I put him in touch with another church in Peterborough, hoping he would go there and that people there would help him.

The following week he called me to tell me that he had gone on Sunday to the church and people had indeed helped him at his point of need. He was being put forward to be housed in a community house with his son, via a project called 'Hope into Action'. He was subsequently accepted, and also joined a small group within that church, and started volunteering to help others in practical ways and this made him feel truly part of a loving, caring family.

One morning recently, however, he was sitting in my consulting room again as I read the discharge letter following an NHS 111 call he had made. Evidently, he was really struggling, which did not surprise me in the least, since the UK had just come out of a 15-month season of social isolation and 'lockdown'. I felt the Holy Spirit nudging me and urging me to invite him to chat about what was going on with him. He had not technically relapsed into addiction, but just felt the need to buy some diazepam off the streets to help with his extreme anxiety and difficulty sleeping.

His son is doing amazingly well, and he is still in touch with the same church, though from a distance, and he sees his parents and sister when he can. So it wasn't clear what was troubling him now, but I felt I should gently probe. It turned out that after all these years he still felt angry and sad over some sustained abuse he suffered in his childhood, part of his tragic and painful past. It was the kind of abuse so difficult to talk about in a family setting, and now that his parents were very elderly and not given to intimate discussions, he felt the matter would forever remain unresolved and undealt with, and he himself would always feel like the black sheep of the family, always 'less than', 'not enough', defective in some way.

I prayed an arrow-type prayer at this point and said to him, 'I think the Father has allowed this to happen today because he wants to deal with this mountain in front of you. You can't go under it and you can't go around it, you must go through it.'

He agreed with me and was keen for me to pray with him, so I invited Holy Spirit to be present and prepare a safe place for him. Then I began to help him engage with the last most painful memory that came to his mind, the time when he felt the smallest, most powerless, and most deeply humiliated.

He was taken surprisingly quickly and easily into that last memory, and was able to relate to me how he had felt in that moment as a boy of ten. He had tears beginning to roll down his face at this point, and I was praying in my mind, my heart racing, and spiritually leaning into the wind! Then I asked Jesus to show him where he, Jesus, was in that memory. The man sat for a while, then said he felt warmth on his shoulders, which became hot. He felt Jesus had his hands on his shoulders. Then he described a face in front of him which was dark, intimidating and evil. After another moment he told me that Jesus had now burnt up the dark face with his 'blazing torch', and the image had disappeared. In its place there was a happy face, innocent and childlike – something like Thomas the Tank Engine, he said. We agreed that this might represent Jesus restoring his innocence and healing some of those childhood wounds, including the pain and shame resulting from past abuse.

But he still felt something lacking within himself and that it was to do with being as a man and a father. I said, 'OK, let's go to another memory, one where you felt most proud and satisfied as a father to your son.' He agreed, and we asked the Holy Spirit to lead. Once again, quite easily, he was able to access that memory, and told me it was when he had presented a gift to his son that he had made himself, a kind of Playstation. He had collected all the parts over a two-year period, and put it all together. His son's had face lit up and he still remembers the emotion of personal joy in that moment. Then I asked the Father to show him where he, the Father, was in that moment.

This time, the man told me that it didn't work at first, until he remembered to pray in his heart and ask God to make it work. Immediately he saw God's presence with him in the memory, and we concluded that Father was always with him, taking pleasure over the creation of this gift, and the giving of it to his son, and was there to make it work! I felt that I could share with him that Father God was clearly reminding him that they can do all of life together and nothing is off God's radar, not the past or the present or the future.

♡ ♡

As I look back on this story, it never fails to amaze me how our conversation with Holy Spirit is heard, every word, and the plight of the poor is known, and every groan, every suffering moment matters to him. I marvel at how he loves to redeem, and at what is possible if we just slow down and stop for the one, and listen to their story.

It's also interesting how in the world of counselling and psychological therapies, it may take years to get to the real wounds, and so to the lies people are living with. Sometimes they are too shut down, or barricaded with walls of defence, to be able to risk dealing with these painful issues. But in the presence of the kindest, wisest, safest counsellor of all, the Holy Spirit, much can be accomplished in a short space of time.

This style of healing ministry has been taught to me through Bethel Sozo UK ministry training workshops. Though it would usually be done in a church-based setting, it can be adapted for anyone in any situation, providing we explain clearly what is going to happen, so that they can understand and give informed consent.

To find out more about this style of healing ministry, visit https://www.bethelsozo.org.uk/

Chapter 6 – Hospital Stories – the Power of Listening

One of the vital skills for a volunteer hospital ward visitor, and one that we are encouraged to go on a course to learn, is that of intentional listening. There is nothing wrong with asking questions, and nothing wrong with having something to say, but listening to another person's story, leaning into their experience, noting the tone of their voice, the expression on their face, picking up their joys and sadnesses, learning what matters to them, is the greatest gift we can give to someone.

When we volunteers were first allowed to return to hospital visiting again during the Covid pandemic, I was allocated a particular ward to visit. It was an orthopaedic /post-surgical ward. Every week, I was able to make a connection to someone, by listening to their story and communicating the Father's love and heart for them. These are a few of those stories, which illustrate the various ways we can use supernatural or prophetic gifts to help any person connect with their Father in heaven.

I always pray that the Lord will lead me to find that one person who is particularly lonely, or in need of some love and special attention. On this occasion I asked the staff if they could think of anyone and they said yes, there was this one little lady in a corner of the ward who was clutching a big stuffed panda, and she was crying all the time, really sad and forlorn. The nurses had tried to comfort her, and said maybe she'd appreciate a visit from me.

So went over and found the lady, and she immediately brightened up as I introduced myself and sat down. I greeted her and the panda warmly and asked what the panda's name was. She declared with impassioned excitement, 'He's forty-seven years old!' Of course, there turned out to be a story behind the panda! Her husband, who had been dead for a long time, had bought it for her on Mother's Day forty-seven years earlier. We went on to chat about all the things she was interested in – she collected stuffed toys and dolls – and we looked at photos on her iPad. At this point I felt the Father say, 'Ask her about her husband.' So I asked her how she met him, and her eyes lit up with joy. 'It was love at first sight,' she said.

She told me the story of how they met at an arcade back in the 1950s, and how he put his tie pin on the lapel on her dress. She said, 'He pinned me! Do you know what that means?'

I said, 'No! Tell me!'

She told me it was the custom back then that a boy would let a girl know he was interested in dating her, and no one else, by fastening his tie pin on her clothing. It was like saying, 'I want you to be my girlfriend. You're the one I'm interested in. Will you go out with me and no one else?'

I was smiling to myself at the thought of this sweet act, when Holy Spirit said to me, 'That's really significant. Hold on to that thought!' So we carried on talking about her life, and most significantly of all, she told me she'd been adopted.

After a while I said I would love to pray for her, and would she let me? 'Oh, yes,' she replied, 'I do pray to the Lord every day,' and she clutched a small crucifix around her neck. Clearly she had a level of faith, and the crucifix suggested that maybe she was a Catholic.

I told her, 'Jesus wants you to know that he's 'pinned' you, and that you belong to him. He's chosen you; you have been adopted into his family, and you are his treasured possession. He will never be separated from you, but always be with you, and will love you forever.'

At this she started to cry, and said 'Open up the drawer next to my bed, and pull out the cardigan.' I did so, and there it was, fastened to her cardigan – the tie pin! All these years later, we were looking at her husband's tie pin, his first act of love towards her. So I symbolically placed the cardigan around her panda and because of the Covid restrictions on patient contact, I held the panda's paw as I prayed for her. The Father connected with her in that moment, letting her know that he had adopted her, and that she was his forever. I prayed for the presence of the Holy Spirit all around the bed, for angels to be present and for healing and wholeness.

When I left the bed a few moments later, she thanked me through her tears, and gave me a beaming smile. She honestly looked radiant!

On another occasion, I asked the nursing staff who they felt would appreciate a chat, and was directed to a lady with the same name as mine, which seemed significant at the time. I had to wait a bit before I could see her, as she had the nurses attending to her when I arrived, and the curtains were drawn around her bed. I chatted to another person for a while, and was almost going to leave that bay, when the curtains were at last pulled back, and there she was!

She had fallen and fractured her spine, and had laid on the floor of her kitchen in terrible pain for eleven hours, before her son-in-law found her and called an ambulance. I was intrigued by her story and by the way she seemed very determined to remain independent, afraid of being a burden to anyone. I felt there was a resistance in her to receiving love, and that she was actually very lonely. Although she lived in an annexe next door to her family, she said that she never ate meals with them or sought their help for fear of getting in their way.

I asked her why she felt so reluctant to ask for help, and she replied that she'd lost her mother when she was twelve and had grown up very fast, needing to manage by herself. It was a pattern she had learned from that time and had never deviated from. Until now.

I asked if I could pray for her, and began to minister to her, focusing particularly on inviting the presence of Jesus, his love and tenderness, to heal her heart and to heal her physically, too. She suddenly stopped me in mid-sentence and began to tell me that she had been in the same hospital with Covid pneumonia six months before. She said she had been unwell for six weeks, sedated or unconscious for much of it, and had nearly died. And one night during that time, she had a 'dream'. She opened her eyes, and felt herself being lifted out of her bed, and floated towards the door of her room. The door opened, and she could see a brilliant light, with many happy faces beyond it, welcoming her. She wanted to go through, but a man came and stood with her at the door, and told her she couldn't come through yet. Then he held her tenderly, and she felt his love all over her body. She was lost in the memory as she told me about it, and I could see her reaction as she remembered that sense of tangible love. It was exactly what she needed. Then she described the man floating with her back to her bed, and saying goodbye. When she woke up from sedation, she quickly began to recover and soon left the hospital.

My hair was standing on end at this point, and I found myself exclaiming, 'That was Jesus!'

She asked my why he would come to her like that, when all her life she had never really made a move towards him. I explained that he loves us so much, he'll come and seek us out. It's never about how worthy we are, he just loves us too much to lose us – it's so simple! I told her he wanted her to know him before it was her time to go, and that she should now believe in him, become a woman of faith! As I left her bedside, there was a warm glow on her face, and a happy smile. A week later I popped into her ward again to visit another person. I checked in on her and found she was now walking and waiting to be discharged.

♡ ♡

This wonderful story illustrates to me that it is so important not to ignore a small nudge from the Holy Spirit. In this case, it was the nudge to linger outside those curtains a bit longer, when I almost gave up and walked away. My time listening intently to the lady's story gave her an opportunity to recall the memory of her dream – an encounter with Jesus that she had no context for or understanding of until that moment.

It needed interpretation, and it needed a willing volunteer to stop and listen to the story and to the heart.

Chapter 7 – Peter

'A bruised reed he will not break, and a smouldering wick he will not snuff out.'
Isaiah 42:3

The following story is one of supernatural interventions, angels of breakthrough and unseen battles for someone's life.

I sat down with Peter in his lounge one day recently and we enjoyed a reunion after a year of not being able to meet up, due to the lockdown and the recent pandemic situation. He looked great – hair a little long and swept back, like an 80s rock star, a good healthy weight, earrings, beads around his wrist, and a radiant smile on his face. Peter is a gentle giant over six feet tall, with searching, light grey eyes, and is one of the kindest, mildest and gentlest people I have ever met.

We reflected happily on the journey he has had to make over the past two and a half years, and the day we first met in my surgery that started his life on a new trajectory. I felt the tangible presence of the Holy Spirit enter the room as he talked in his mild tone of voice, unhurried, sincere, with every word carefully considered. He shared his perspective on what had happened and what he had learnt, and I was moved to tears, particularly when he shared what he felt God had shown him through the intensity of his adversity.

Peter is the father of four children, the youngest aged three, and he lives independently from his ex-partner, a mutual decision made years ago. He loves the children dearly and remains involved in their lives and, when he can, he volunteers at the homeless project in town where he loves to love the broken. Peter is one of those people about whom Jesus spoke when he said, 'Blessed are the meek, for they will inherit the kingdom of God' (Matthew 5:5). He owns very little, is content with what he has, and demands absolutely nothing from anyone. I felt like I was on holy ground that day, and the Holy Spirit had me kneel down and pray for him, placing my hands on his painful neuropathic feet, for healing and anointing... for happy feet!

I first met Peter in October 2018. I was looking through my clinic letter inbox, when I noticed a discharge letter from the hospital about a man who had been sent there by one of my colleagues, concerned that he appeared 'emaciated, and very unwell'. In the hospital he was given antibiotics, checked over, then sent home. Immediately I sensed that I was to meet with him, and look after him more intentionally. So I called him, and asked him if he wanted to come down for a face-to-face appointment, to which he happily agreed.

Peter at that time was malnourished, pale, hollow-faced, and indeed looked very unwell. I asked him about his situation, and discovered he was homeless, living in his car, parking up wherever he could. He had chronic lung disease, and was avoidant of medical services on the whole, shutting down and withdrawing into himself, due to paralysing fear.

Peter remembers more clearly than me all that I said to him that day, as he sat in the Mercy Seat, but I do remember that I said, 'You are so worthy to be loved – did you know that?' He remembers that I prayed for him, and referred him to the 'Garden House Project' in the cathedral grounds, a brand-new homeless project at the time. I gave him the name of a wonderful friend of mine, Chrissy, who was part of the team pioneering the project, and told him firmly that he was to go there in the morning and ask her to help him.

The next day I was volunteering there myself on my day off, and the doorbell rang – it was Peter standing at the door looking for Chrissy! We welcomed him in, and made so much fuss over him, and showered love on him in every way we knew how. He was interviewed by the housing officer, and very quickly he was offered first stage accommodation. That morning he became a believer in Jesus, and opened his life up completely, a simple faith was born, and within a short time, strong bonds were forged with all the team, volunteers and the other clients. We prayed for him every week, and Jesus began to release him gradually from all of his mental torment, which was rooted in trauma and rejection at a young age.

Within a few weeks, Peter was painting buildings on the grounds, making coffees for clients and interviewing them. He was family and everyone on the project has always loved him. He was later baptised in the Cathedral, and became part of the pastoral care side of the homeless ministry at the Garden House.

Fast forward a year, and I was no longer volunteering at the project, but was still caring for Peter as his GP, though I hadn't heard anything from him for a long time. I bumped into him one day, on my day off, in the city centre. I was in the bank and he just wandered in. I knew it was a divine appointment, as he told me he had no idea why he just felt compelled to go into the bank! I asked him how he was feeling, and he replied, not so good. In fact, he was very thirsty, losing weight and feeling very fatigued. I got him to come down to the surgery the next day and did his blood test myself. There were ketones showing in his urine, and I realised he had developed diabetes and was in danger of imminent dehydration.

My plan was to admit him to hospital as soon as I got his test result. However, the crucial result didn't come back because the lab rejected the sample, due the bottle being out of date. Can you imagine the frustration? I tried to get him to come back, but the next day I couldn't get him to answer his phone. Over the weekend I worried about him, and prayed for him. By Monday he still wasn't answering his phone and I imagined him in a coma all weekend. It turned out that he had moved house and not informed the practice of his new address. I tried the Garden House Project team, but no one had seen or heard from him in a few weeks, and they didn't know his new address either!

That day for me was the worst day of my GP career. I wanted that address so badly, that I decided to drive into the city centre in the middle of my working day to find someone on the Project who knew where Peter lived. Eventually I called Chrissy, who was away on holiday, and she gave me his new address. I called the GP who looks after the clients who attend the Project, and she agreed to call the police, as this was clearly a medical emergency. At six o'clock that Monday evening, they broke into Peter's house and found him deeply comatosed and hypothermic. The paramedics thought he must have taken an overdose, but we were able to tell them that this he was in a diabetic ketoacidotic coma, and he needed critical care admission immediately. We prayed all night and all the next day for Peter, contending for his life.

I saw him once in critical care with Chrissy, and met his parents there that day as well. I was heartbroken to see our gentle giant struggling for his every breath, his eyes glazed over, as he was barely able to register our presence in the room.

He remained in critical care for four weeks, and in hospital for another month. His kidneys failed, and he required dialysis. Many of us were praying earnestly for him, and I felt Holy Spirit ask me one day to go to the ward and visit him and pray for his kidneys. After I'd done this, I monitored his renal function at work, as I was able to access the hospital system from the GP surgery. His numbers just kept improving, and a week later he was no longer needing dialysis. Peter told me today that he knew it was nothing less than a miracle, as the consultant had told him he was planning to send him to Leicester to get a special shunt put in his arm, ready for long term haemodialysis.

He then spent three months in an intermediate care facility, learning to walk again, as he had lost just about all of his muscle bulk from weeks of being in bed. He also needed to learn how to manage his diabetes with insulin. He was isolated from most friends, as this was the time of the pandemic and no visitors were allowed. Despite all this, His faith and courage did not fail. He loves to see the bright side of every situation, and he maintains that he received so much love and care from the staff, both in hospital and in the intermediate care facility, that it changed his life.

When I saw him again recently, we reflected on all of this, and we both marvelled at the grace of God; the Mercy Seat where Peter initially sat, the divine appointment at the bank, the way he had been delivered in the nick of time from dying alone in his house, and the measure of supernatural healing in his body under the amazing care of the hospital team – a beautiful example of God working through the combination of both natural and supernatural means of healing.

He says he believes he now knows the heart of God so well, that he is full of compassion for the homeless people he meets. He says that he sees people differently now, and even the most needy and unusual people he meets remind him of how valuable people are, and he has radically changed in his outlook on this broken world.

♡ ♡

As I look back on this story, it fills me with memories of supernatural interventions, divine appointments, timing down to the wire, but also of terrifying possibility of loss of life or quality of life due to delays and mistakes made on a human level. But God was at work here, cancelling every assignment against Peter's life, showing himself to be the defender of the weak, and father of the fatherless. Truly he is the one who gets us the breakthrough when we cry out to him.

I think this taught me about the unseen realms and the spiritual battles we are in as healthcare professionals, and as those seeking to bring God's kingdom into uncharted territory where Jesus wants us to declare his rule and reign. It taught me that at times we will need to contend for what we are believing for, and that there is risk involved. I have found reassurance and strength in the following scriptures, which give us an understanding of this unseen battle, and clear indication that we are supported by heavenly armies and the presence of Jesus who is with us, to help us overcome: 2 Chronicles 20:17, John 16:33.

We are indeed at war, but the battles are his, not ours, and he allows us to partner with him in his victory! Life will always be filled with excitement and surprises when we understand it from this perspective.

I also want to draw attention to the childlike faith of one man who faced death several times, and has really suffered huge amounts of physical pain and loss. He is one of the unseen heroes of the faith and his heavenly Father and all of heaven are proud of him. He is a stunning example for me to follow and I thank God for having brought him into my life and allowed me to know him.

Chapter 8 – The Power of Testimony

'Jesus in a bar? What about Jesus in a doctor's surgery?'

As I switched on my computer one morning, after a busy week, I felt a nudge from the Holy Spirit to stop for a moment and listen to a WhatsApp message – a video testimony, sent from a friend a few days previously, but which I hadn't yet had the space and time to listen to.

It was entitled, 'Jesus in a bar' and was the testimony of a musician called Chris Burns. As I listened, I was mesmerised for those few minutes. Chris was making an album of live worship music which had taken place during a recent revival, in a bar on a boulevard in New Orleans! The story he told was that of a bar owner, searching for meaning and purpose, who had a revelatory dream, in which Jesus appeared to him and said, ' Hey, it's me – Jesus – I am real!' The bar owner said to Jesus, 'Lord, I will give up my bar and follow you,' whereupon Jesus replied, 'No, don't do that – I have need of it!'

After that, he invited Chris Burns down to lead worship in the bar for a season, and so many people were attracted in by the sound of worship and revival, that they were overflowing into the street outside. There were baptisms, ministry, healings, deliverances – all happening during these gatherings, right there in Bourbon Street, New Orleans!

As I was pondering this, I looked through the list to see who was wanting a call back that morning, and saw the name of a lady I have been supporting for a long time, trying to help get some level of breakthrough for her mental health and wellbeing. Nothing I had tried with regard to her medication had helped her much, and none of my motivational material, verbal encouragements, or words of wisdom had given her any level of breakthrough. Her anxiety, brokenness, and fears all remained entrenched. I found myself internally praying and saying to Jesus, 'OK, I've just heard about Jesus in a bar – how about Jesus in a doctor's surgery right now?'

During our consultation I was praying in my heart for a word of knowledge or wisdom, and I felt I needed to ask her, 'Who do you most need to forgive?' She immediately replied, 'My Dad!' As she explained, I saw clearly that the father wounds in her heart did indeed run deep. She was very angry with him for his neglect and all the pain of absence and detachment, lack of validation, and harshness towards her all her life.

I shared with her the connection between emotional pain, anger, unforgiveness and mental health issues. I then explained what forgiveness actually is, and how in releasing her father from her judgments on him, she would be releasing herself, too. She understood and agreed but said, 'I just don't know how!'

After a little more Holy Spirit prompting, I began to share with her my own journey, finding my faith and living as a daughter of God, attached to his heart for me and healed by his kindness and love, and so able to do really difficult things with his help. Still even with this understanding she was standing on the edge of a decision, and was paralysed in her mind, unable to take the next step.

So at this point I offered to pray with her and asked her if she would like to encounter Jesus herself and ask for his help in forgiving her dad. She readily agreed, so I led her line by line in a prayer. First, we looked at the untruths she believed about her lack of worth and lack of ability to change her circumstances. Then we spoke our acknowledgement that these things were untrue, and expressed aloud the breaking of any agreement with them. Then we spoke words of truth about her identity, agreeing with Father's opinion of her. She then asked him to come into her life, and help her know how to be his daughter. Finally, we contemplated the image of the cross for a moment and I prayed that she might see the depth of pain and shame that Jesus experienced as he hung on the cross, and how much he was willing to forgive all of us.

She prayed with me to forgive her dad, handing him over to Jesus, and knowing he also has his own pain to deal with. As she prayed each line, concentrating hard, her voice got stronger, and her understanding of what she was saying seemed to me to be increasing. At that moment the presence of God was so strong in the room that when she got up to leave, she actually felt quite wobbly, then started laughing and smiling, tears rolling down her face. She embraced me and thanked me, full of gratitude and wonderment at what just happened! My own wonderment remained after she had left the room! She had just encountered Jesus in a doctor's surgery, and Jesus had fulfilled his promise: 'You may ask me for anything in my name and I will do it.' (John 14 v 14)

In that moment I saw God do something I have never seen him do before, at least, not directly with me in my role as a healthcare professional. But it seems that he already knew exactly what he wanted to do, and set me up with the courage and faith I needed by having me listen to an extraordinary testimony beforehand. Here was the example of the power of the testimony! When we hear about a miraculous intervention, we can either choose to distance ourselves and be unaffected by it, or say, this is what I want to see happen again, right here and now! He is more than willing to show up for us when we apprehend his goodness and allow him to repeat the miracle.

Finally, this story illustrates again the mercy and compassion and deep knowledge he has for people, it just blows my mind every time. Honestly I am beginning to see that there is no darkness, no hopelessness, no place of despair that is immune from the presence of God.

Chapter 9 – Healing Miracles

'People ask, "Is it legitimate to be asking for signs and wonders, miracles?" I say, "If you find his hand, you just need to look up to find his face – it's never far away".'

Bill Johnson

My wonderfully courageous, intelligent, articulate and tenacious eighty-eight-year-old lady patient was crying on the phone. She always knew what to do, what to ask for, how to handle herself, but on this occasion the strength she so often relied on had failed her. Her knee revision surgery, which she and I had battled for three years to get done, had finally taken place eleven weeks before, but the wound had not healed.

She had been going to the local hospital's orthopaedic clinic to see her surgeon weekly for eight weeks, for inspection and re-dressing. The surgeon had told her that her arterial circulation was so bad in that leg that the wound could not heal, and she would most likely end up needing an above knee amputation. Those words fell on her like the final curtain at the end of a tragic play. All this waiting and suffering, all for nothing.

I decided it was time to visit her in her own home, take a look at the wound, and spend some time listening to her story. As I drove over to her house, I thought to myself, and it was only a fleeting thought, 'I could pray for her. I have never even asked her about her faith, and she doesn't seem the sort of person to easily talk about spirituality.' But when I arrived, she let me in, and even before I could sit down, she asked me 'Dr Cronau, before we talk further, I must just ask you – are you a spiritualist?'

'Well,' I said, laughing in surprise at such a bizarre greeting, 'No, I'm not a spiritualist, but I am spiritual. I am a Christian!' She said, 'Good! Because I need one, I'm not getting anywhere with this knee and I need a miracle!'

When I asked her why she had said this, she told me that a friend in her housing complex, also a patient of mine, had told her that I was a spiritual person! That lady was someone I had once prayed with and shared worship songs with in her flat during a home visit, and I had also encouraged her with a little prophetic word over the phone, around the meaning of her name. (Three patients with the same name had come up three times on the screen, which drew my attention to it, and the Holy Spirit prompted me to look up the meaning and share it with her. It meant 'light and joy'!)

So I sat down, took off the leg brace she was supposed to wear to keep her leg straight, and peeled the pus-soaked dressing away carefully, revealing a macerated wound about seven inches long and widely separating in three places, with no evidence of good new healing tissue, that we call granulation tissue. She was unable to walk or weight-bear properly, and was thoroughly miserable.

I was praying under my breath, 'Lord, what do you want to do this time?' And I felt him say, 'Just do what's in front of you, then pray for a miracle!'

So we placed over the wound a piece of leftover non-adherent dressing given to her from the hospital. It didn't cover the whole thing, just the three areas where the wound was still open. I prescribed her a course of antibiotics, told her not to wear the brace, and to go to her hospital re-dressing appointment on the Thursday. Then I prayed for her. She is very hard of hearing, even with hearing aids, so I knelt down and spoke clearly and simply. 'Lord, let your healing come upon this knee wound right now, and let this leg be saved. Bring back the circulation, let there never have to be an amputation, but a fully functional leg, and heal all the places of disappointment in her heart throughout this whole time of suffering.'

After I left, I wondered at the way the Lord had set me up for this, and how the time was perfect for a miracle. I had unusual faith for this, and

I felt I should ask a dear intercessor friend for her prayers for a miracle for this lady.

On the Thursday, towards lunchtime, the lady rang and told me, 'I had to let you know – it's amazing, I can't believe it – it's all but healed! I've just come back from the hospital. The consultant couldn't believe it either!'

You can imagine how happy I was to hear this, and it would have been enough that Jesus had touched this lady with physical healing, but he had so much more in store for her.

Soon she was on the phone again, and this time she described feelings of sadness, tearfulness, low mood, and just being 'not herself'. Again, I felt I needed to visit her in her home, and this time I felt the Lord tell me to listen to her life story. It was an amazing story, a life filled with adventure, travel, living in Zimbabwe in southern Africa, amongst other places. There were losses and bereavements, dangers, loneliness, and triumphs. She really is a most wonderfully interesting and courageous lady.

I sensed that she had been traumatised during her time in the care home she was sent to for convalescence after her knee revision surgery, during the pandemic lockdown. She ended up being there for five weeks, with no visitors, and could still hear inside her head the echoes of screaming and agitated elderly residents all around her, many of them suffering from dementia. She felt the heavy weight of the loneliness, and the fear of losing her mind and independence, and perhaps living out her days in a care home herself eventually. The words of the consultant also played on her mind, 'You'll probably end up needing an amputation.'

I began to speak to her about her heavenly Father, how he loved her adventurous spirit, and how he had been with her all through her adventures and was still, in this season of her life, wanting connection with her. He had healed her knee wound, but wanted to heal her heart as well. So I prayed for her, and we spoke about eternity, heaven and all kinds of other things that were on her mind. The presence of God was really strong in her flat that day, and she still asks me to pray for her whenever she comes to the surgery for anything. She says, 'It does me so much good when you pray,' and 'He really is a God of miracles!'

When I reflect on this story, the thing that stands out is sometimes people just need a physical healing miracle, which in the presence of faith God is well able to do. I also learnt that he helps us know when it is the right time to ask for that, and he sets up divine clues like a treasure map! I also believe that after the miracle takes place a person is ready to open their eyes and look up at Jesus, and encounter his love for them. There is always more he wants to heal than just a part of our physical body. He is longing for connection with every person and every miracle sets them up for an invitation to meet him. What a joy to be part of this process!

Chapter 10 – Burnt Stones

'The Sovereign Lord has given me a well-instructed tongue, to know the word that sustains the weary. He wakens me morning by morning, wakens my ear to listen like one being instructed.'
Isaiah 50:3-4

The power of the Word of God
One morning before I went to work, I was reading Nehemiah chapters 3 and 4, which are all about the rebuilding of the gates and walls of Jerusalem – each man, woman and child making the needed repairs either near to their home, or on an assigned section of the wall. I thought to myself, 'I will be rebuilding a little piece of the wall today.'

The passage goes on to describe the ridicule that Nehemiah faced from his opponents, who taunted him, saying, 'Will they restore their wall? … Can they bring the stones back to life from those heaps of rubble – burned as they are?' (Nehemiah 4:2)

The picture of those stones captured my heart. I imagined them blackened with soot and ruined in the fire. I was reminded how people are to God like living stones, and beautiful, but they get tarnished, burnt and blackened by the relentless attrition of life's difficult circumstances, painful relationship betrayals, etc, until they feel as if they have been thrown away into the rubble, figuratively speaking, useless for anything.

I sensed that God wanted me to pick up these 'burnt stones' carefully, attentively, one at a time and help restore them, so they can be placed back into in their allotted place in society, in families, homes and jobs.

There was one lady that day that I felt to stop for. She rang up saying that she felt desperately 'mentally ill' as she put it. She said she was anxious, not coping, and self-harming. So I said to her, 'Come on in, let's have a chat about it all'.

Her story turned out to be one of awful childhood abuse, and the context for the start of all her problems. The roots of her 'mental illness' lay in trauma, as is so often the case. As I listened to her, I found myself praying silently to Holy Spirit. 'Lord, what can we do to help this lady know her value and worth in the face of such brokenness?' He immediately gave me some wisdom and a strategy for her.

I got her to list all the people who had hurt her, and to unburden herself right there of all her grievances against them. We wrote it all down, and then I tasked her to find time and space later to express all her feelings, so as to release all the toxicity of those negative emotions from her body and mind. Then I used a tool often used in counselling methods, but so powerful in this context, which is to imagine all the people and their associated offences in a boat, and to imagine letting the boat go, and visualising them drifting off to their own destinies. To my amazement she was able to engage with this and really let some of these offences go in that moment. I began to share with her who she really was, and could now become, because she had chosen to let go of some of the burden she was carrying around.

She was amazed, and we ended a potentially really difficult consultation with a majorly positive outcome, and I could discern that she had turned a corner in her life. I also spoke to her about the postcards on my wall, which all refer to a woman's worth, beauty and significance. I told her that she needed to have good things put back in, as all the toxic beliefs she held about herself were now going to be relinquished, and this was basically rooted in the fact that she was loved, and that her true identity in God's eyes was that of a daughter and a princess.

♡ ♡

I was really thankful that day for the fresh word of God in my heart, and the ability to just listen to the impulses he gave me in the heat of the moment. He always shows up when we take a risk, and engage our hearts to see his kingdom come. People each have their identity and assignments in life allotted by their loving Creator and heavenly Father, but the enemy loathes people getting any measure of freedom and dignity, or getting cleaned up and picked up out of the rubble of life. He will always discourage us from even trying to pick up these 'burnt stones', telling us they are too heavy, too ruined, too far gone. It's a terrible lie, and one we need to contend against as healthcare professionals and healers. God has given us tools of wisdom and knowledge to combat these lies, and in reality we are in a battle. We are on the front line, each of us making the repairs around our allotted part of the wall of our society or community, doing our part in rebuilding the kingdom, lifting up the broken-hearted, restoring those 'burnt stones'.

I feel like I am learning to see from God's perspective that far from this being an overwhelmingly negative and tragic season of continual increasing lack and loss, it is really more a day of unprecedented opportunity!

Chapter 11 – Blessing the Unseen

Every Christmas for years, I would leave an invitation for the Kingsgate Church Christmas guest service out for Maggie, one of our cleaning staff, who cleaned my room each night.

Maggie was tiny in stature, well past retirement age, and frail with a kyphosis (curvature) of her spine. She also had emphysema of her lungs, frequent bouts of bronchitis, and a broken knee replacement in one of her knees desperately needing revision surgery. Despite all this she was determined, hardworking, diligent and faithful, never missing a shift. She was a joy to see at the end of a busy day, and if I worked late she would come into my room to see if it was vacant and ready to clean. After a while, I felt God wanted to bless her and I was moved to leave her little gifts and cards of appreciation every once in a while. If it was near to Christmas or Easter, I would leave an invitation to the guest services as well.

She didn't ever come to those guest services, because she suffered from anxiety, and would feel awkward about asking for a lift or being in the company of strangers in that unfamiliar setting. Maggie didn't go out anywhere for pleasure. She worked three jobs, the other two being in schools, one as a cleaner, the other as a lunchtime supervisor. Her life revolved around labouring to provide for her family, and trying to keep busy. Engaging with work gave her meaning and purpose, and she loved to please and serve others.

Gradually I became more bold, and I offered to pray for her knee, which was swollen and causing her to limp profoundly. She would maintain that it felt better after prayer, but I never saw any improvement if I'm honest. So she agreed eventually to let me take her to the 'Healing Rooms', a ministry which takes place at Kingsgate Church every Monday evening. It is a walk-in prayer healing ministry, run by people who are full of compassion, and very prophetically anointed.

That evening she shared her story with me as we waited for her turn for prayer – how her marriage had ended, how her father was never much involved in her life, how she became the sole provider for her children in every way, and how her Catholic faith was real, but she really had no personal connection to Father God, or to Jesus as her lover and healer. She opened her heart to him and gave her life to him that night, as well as receiving prayer for healing for her knee. I will always remember her delight and her laughter as we drove home, how it all made sense to her now, and how she had felt God's presence in that time of prayer.

She was given a Bible by someone in Kingsgate Church who later took her there a couple of times. Now, in the evenings after work, if I met her in the corridor, she would call me over to the closet where all the cleaning stuff is stored, and share with me how she had read the Bible, and ask me questions. I could now leave her little messages, with words of encouragement and truths about her identity as a daughter which she loved to receive. I often prayed with her for her issues, and she was always up for a hug!

Maggie was someone who was reluctant to seek help in any way for anything. One evening she told me she had been having some rectal bleeding symptoms. I was horrified to learn of this as it can signify rectal cancer, and she had ignored it for more than three months already. When she eventually got her GP to refer her and get a diagnosis, it became apparent that it was indeed cancer. It was agonising for me to learn of this easily treatable disease being allowed to take hold of her already frail body.

Whilst she was in hospital, I went to visit her, and we played worship songs through my phone and I prayed for her. I also visited her once at home with our practice manager and tried to cheer her up and make her aware she was missed and a valuable part of the team.

But things just got worse as her condition progressed, and one morning I received a message from her daughter saying that she had died in the night, at home, without anyone present and with no one really aware that she was so near the end of her life.

I was heartbroken, and I can honestly say that the way she died deeply impacted me. It was difficult to concentrate that morning, but I just tried to work through my caseload that day as best as I could. It made me feel sad at how life just carries on when people we love leave us, even if they were a significant part of our lives. New cleaning staff had already taken Maggie's place, and no one really even knew her story, or anything about her last illness, except me and our manager. The daily routine just relentlessly carried on. But Jesus knew and loved her, he valued her, he saw her, met with her and was with her at the end, when nobody else was there. And he has now given her a brand-new body, free of deformity and pain.

Her funeral was held on a cold day during the Covid lockdown. The doors were left open for ventilation, and all of us were sitting quietly, distanced from each other, wrapped up in warm coats, lost in our own thoughts. But I felt God's presence strongly there, in the quiet sanctuary of the church, and I became aware of, and wondered at, the beautiful, dignifying ministry of the Catholic priests. They presided over the service diligently, acknowledging Maggie and her children, working together seamlessly. The readings were packed with Scriptures referring to eternal life, and the hope that Jesus gives us beyond our physical existence. And I wondered just what she would be enjoying now.

I am so thankful to the Father for the way he had me stop for Maggie, because she was his treasured possession from the start. Once she knew that truth in reality, her joy knew no bounds. I believe it carried her in hope through all her pain and suffering right up to the end of her life. Later her daughter came in to speak to me about her own faith journey, which had been until now buried under life's challenges and busyness. She felt that her mother had given her a legacy that she wanted to explore and take her own journey of faith discovery. She is a very different person from her mother, and has a very different life story to tell, and I was able to pray with her about this at a subsequent bereavement consultation.

I am excited to see what that journey might turn out to be.

Chapter 12 – When Sorrow is Overwhelmed by Compensation

'If I ever want to feel close to Jesus, I just go and hang out with the poor, because that's where he hangs out. If I keep showing up I'll find him there, because there's always someone broken to love on and to call out hope for them, to speak life over them'
Unknown

The story of Eunice
I had never met Eunice before, but the moment I heard about her through my colleague, who randomly popped into my room for a chat and felt like telling me about her awful CT scan results, I knew that God wanted to minister to her through me. My colleague was about to depart for India for some time to see his family, and was not going to be around for the foreseeable future, so I took on the task of looking after this lady during his absence. I called her and invited her down to the surgery.

It was a massive liver tumour, with background liver cirrhosis, and hepatitis B positive status. She had come to the surgery feeling unwell, tired out and losing weight only a few weeks before. She was thirty years old.

When she first came to see me, she was unaware of her diagnosis and completely shut down –vague, uncommunicative, barely able to speak. She seemed unable to comprehend what I was saying to her, as I tried to make her aware of the gravity of the situation, without causing her to lose hope. I did not know whether she was having a strong emotional response to this serious illness, perhaps some kind of shock, or was in denial, or whether the disease was perhaps directly affecting her brain, as there were already widespread metastatic deposits of tumour in her body.

I told her I was a Christian and that I would be praying for her, whereupon she immediately brightened up and told me she too was a believer. We prayed together, asking Jesus into her situation, to help her battle this illness, and make his presence known to her – to be to her now, what he couldn't be to her in any other situation.

The following week, she was admitted to A&E with chest pains and breathlessness, and was found to have, in addition to everything else, a heart condition called Cardiomyopathy, which in itself was advanced and seriously life-altering. It was hard to fathom this sudden devastating series of events in this young woman's life. Out of the blue, she was facing a very short life prognosis, and was completely unprepared, unsupported and disengaged with the medical system. Eunice lived with her mother, who spoke very little English, and a brother who was rarely at home. Her father was caught up in Covid restrictions and stuck in Italy, where they had previously lived as an intact family. He also was sick with an advanced intractable neurological illness, Huntingdon's disease, and not expected to live long. The whole situation seemed utterly hopeless.

I decided to visit Eunice's home, which turned out to be a three-storey council town house, with steep stairs up to the first-floor lounge, and more stairs up to the bedroom level. I spent a long time ringing the bell and knocking on the door before her mother, a tiny, frail, elderly Ghanaian lady, let me in. She led me upstairs, where I found Eunice lying on a tatty old settee. This had become her makeshift bed, as she could not negotiate the stairs by this point. There was hardly any furniture, and my heart sank as I realised the difficulty of helping her through this illness in these circumstances. Her mother, now the sole breadwinner, was out during the day, working as a cleaner.

By the end of this visit I had a plan. In addition to medication, our surgery team would support her, we would get a hospital bed delivered, district nurses would visit to monitor her, and we would request a MacMillan nurse. We got all this set up quickly for her. Some steroid medication seemed to brighten her up almost immediately, making her much more lucid and, for the time being, pain free. The hospital, meanwhile, reluctantly agreed to discuss chemotherapy. Eunice was keen to try it, though her frail body would have a tough time suffering the side effects. It would be palliative chemotherapy, the blanket type not designed to cure, but to prolong life for a short time.

The following week, I returned with a huge bunch of flowers, a vase, and a large tin of tropical fruit. Eunice, her mother and I stood together and prayed, asking the presence of God to come, and the kingdom of heaven to invade this hellish disease. The presence of Jesus was tangible, and I was moved at how open they were, a powerful, uncomplicated, unoffended spirit of faith rising up in them.

She loved to worship, and the one thing they did possess was a TV, and so she was able to listen to worship songs on YouTube. So I introduced her to Maverick City and other current worship leaders who loved the presence of God. I brought her some pillows one day, just wanting to drop them off, but her mother implored me to come upstairs to see her, because she said my visits made her happy.

The final time I visited Eunice, she was much weaker, and the tumour was now so advanced that there was no time for any treatment intervention. We talked about how she was feeling, and prayed together one last time. While I was praying, she put on a worship song and we just stayed for some moments in God's presence. It was all that was needed now. One of the songs I had given her was Naomi Raine, singing 'Find my peace'.

Come near to me, closer to me, Jesus,
Don't let me go, no other help I know, Jesus.
Jesus, come fight for me, you make the darkness flee, Jesus.
I know I can't do anything, as you strengthen me, Jesus.

So when the enemy comes to lie to me, I will not fear because you've
prayed for me.
I find my peace in you, Jesus,
All of my joy in you, Jesus.

Eunice was under the care of an amazing MacMillan nurse colleague,
who happens also to be a faith-filled believer. She arranged for her to
be admitted in good time to our local hospice. Her Mum and brother
were there when she took her last breath. She was surrounded by caring
professionals, a lovely atmosphere, and her nearest relatives. I thank
God for the way he provided comfort and dignity as he ushered her into
her new body and her new kingdom home. Her joy and worship know
no bounds now, no more fear of losing or leaving or missing out. Her
compensation is what he has prepared for her from the beginning of
the world.

I visited her mother one last time, with bright colourful daisies, for
her to be reminded of where Mavis is now. She showed me with pride
the beautiful dress she had bought for Eunice to be dressed in for the
funeral, and it was hard to hold back the tears. We just stood and hugged
for a long time, and with the brother there I asked him to translate what
words I could bring to comfort her.

One month later the father, who had managed to come to England,
but missed his daughter's passing, died himself in our local hospital.

When I think of this family, my heart just breaks, but I think back to the
words of that song, and how Jesus himself is our great compensation,
and in the end the only thing that lasts is not our mortal bodies, our
homes and possessions, our achievements or earthly aspirations, but
our big adventure of eternal life with him.

I pray that anyone reading this, who feels emotional because of losing their loved one, perhaps in some similar circumstances, may be comforted just as Eunice and her mother have been. His mercy has made bountiful provision for everything we will ever need... for ever.

Chapter 13 – A Hand on the Shoulder

Sometimes people in my consultations get much more than they bargained for!

I had booked this particular chap in for a knee injection. He had developed really advanced osteoarthritis in his knees at a relatively young age, and it was affecting his work life, his mood and his emotional wellbeing. He was only in his fifties. I have always sensed a gentleness about him. He is softly spoken, goes out of his way to express gratitude, and is very polite and considerate, and remarkably uncomplaining, considering his problems.

As he came in the door, I asked him how he was doing, and without hesitation he said, 'Not very well really, my mother has just died.' He began to tear up, and look down at the ground.

I was already running late at the end of a very busy surgery, and was set up to go ahead with his injection, but I noted what he said about his bereavement and thought to myself, 'Maybe we'll get a chance to talk about this afterwards.'

So after his injection, as he went to leave, I asked him, in a way I wouldn't normally ask, 'Is there any trauma relating to your mum's death that you would like to talk about today, and leave behind?' It's not the normal way I would approach bereavement, but there just seemed to be an atmosphere of freedom and permission for authenticity in the room that morning.

Sure enough, he started to talk about the emotional storm that he was experiencing in the wake of his mother passing away. She had evidently never been kind to him; in fact, she was extremely harsh and apparently favoured his sisters over him from when he was very young. He mentioned how she would often unfairly chastise him, beat him, tug on his hair, etc. He was utterly traumatised in his childhood, and even now, thinking about her as an eighty-year-old woman brought tears to his eyes. He said, 'My sisters lost a mother they loved. I have lost a mother I never knew or felt close to.'

He was also bullied at school and developed an aggressive strategy of self-defence, becoming quite a fighter into adulthood, and constantly worrying that his suppressed anger might flare up if anyone confronted him aggressively.

I have a folder containing cognitive behavioural therapy 'tools' that I use in different contexts with different people. One of these 'tools' is a piece of blackened card with words painted on it in red of negative or toxic emotions that people may experience, but not necessarily consciously realise they are carrying inside them. The words include anger, rage, bitterness, regret, remorse, loneliness, disappointment, among others. I got this out, showed it to the man and asked him which ones he related to the most.

'All of them!' he replied. And as he began to unpack his stories, they flowed from him, one after the other, like a torrent breaking through a dam. There was so much trauma – a lifetime, it seemed, of holding these feelings inside himself.

He said, 'I've never told this to anyone, ever,' and I realised he was in a very vulnerable place with me, and I sensed the Holy Spirit in the room. The man was in the Mercy Seat.

I asked him if he would like to leave some of these emotions behind, to which he replied yes.

We chose to focus on a particular memory relating to his mother's cruelty towards him. I explained to him how we were going to imagine her and her actions in a boat, tethered to him by a rope that he was holding onto and which was exhausting him. It represented him holding her to account, and holding onto the pain and disappointments. He engaged quite well, but I felt it wasn't enough and that I needed to give the Holy Spirit something more to work with for his healing.

So I just told him, as he sat there with his eyes closed, 'I am a Christian, and I am sensing that Father God is standing behind you with his arm around you, his hand on your shoulders. I sense that he wants you to know he loves you, is proud of you and it's all going to be ok. You can now let go, and He wants to heal your heart.'

At this he opened his eyes, and began telling me something that was clearly very important to him. At the moment I said, 'I am a Christian,' he had a memory of when he was much younger, and his father had collapsed and died at home in front of him, probably with a heart attack. The young boy had been devastated, and at the same time terrified, but at that moment he had felt a hand on his shoulder, and heard a voice speaking into his ear, saying, 'Don't worry, I am with you and it's going to be OK'. His sister, he said, told him later that she had seen a flash of light around him! 'I'm not a bible basher or churchgoer or anything like that,' he said, 'but since then I have always believed in God. How did you know?'

I was utterly amazed, and was able to explain that it was the Holy Spirit who directed me to say these things, because he is present, knows him, loves him and wants to connect with him still after all these years. He left the room feeling known, seen and loved, and I do believe some of his suffering and pain was relieved.

Once again, it was a divine set-up, and I have to admit I almost missed it, but the kindness of God allowed me not to stumble over the opportunity.

Recently, I spoke with the man again and discovered that after that consultation he had gone to see his sister and had a heart-to-heart conversation with her. He talked to her about many of his traumatic experiences during their shared childhood, and found her sympathetic and understanding. He told me that he now feels a tremendous peace and a sense of closure.

♡ ♡

I think this story reminds me about how important it is to notice people's emotional reactions to the questions we ask. The Holy Spirit is often the one who is waiting to help the person unburden themselves, but they are unaware of what they are carrying around. Once again there is a soft place, where all the barriers can come down, and God can make a connection with the person in the most natural of ways, leaving them feeling safe, loved, known and seen. We just need to 'see' them first!

Chapter 14 – Unravelling a Bereavement

'The spirit of the Sovereign Lord is upon me, because the Lord
has anointed me to proclaim good news to the poor. He has sent
me to bind up the broken-hearted, to proclaim freedom for the
captives, to proclaim the year of the Lord's favour... to comfort all
who mourn, and provide for those who grieve.'
Isaiah 6:1-3

This lady had called in desperation, feeling the lowest she could ever
imagine feeling, and even struggling with thoughts of suicide, which
had begun to seem like a sweet relief and escape from all her sadness.

I knew her to be a hard-working, quite brilliant professional leader
in her field, who had just started a promising new job. I sensed from
the Holy Spirit that we needed to meet, so I asked her if she'd like to
come in immediately, which she readily agreed to. It seemed like an
urgent assignment.

She told me that a month earlier, her mother had died quite suddenly
in her homeland of Australia, after a short, unexpected illness.
Her mother had been her main source of strength, affirmation and
unconditional love. They had been best friends and talked every day for
years, even after she moved to the UK, but she was unable to travel to
Australia to be with her mother in her last days, because of the pandemic
restrictions on travel. In addition to this loss, her father seemed to be
quickly comforted and consoled by the affections of another woman,
not known to her mother. Her brother, who had never left Australia, had
lashed out in his pain, accusing her of abandoning her family years ago,
and leaving him to care for their mother alone. To complete this picture
of desolation, she had just gone through an acrimonious divorce after
twenty years of unhappy marriage to a man who could not show love or
meet her need for affection.

As she told me her story, we were able to identify some of the wounds and lies that had accumulated over time, especially the false guilt she had picked up from her brother, and the disappointment with her father's apparent insensitivity and disloyalty in so quickly forming a relationship with another woman.

We talked honestly about suicide, and how it can feel like a real option in these impossibly dark circumstances, when we feel overwhelmed and have no more strength to fight with. We talked through the fact that it is, in fact, the worst option, because it is passing on the pain to others. We talked about the importance of leaving a legacy, firstly her mother's legacy to her, and then secondly her own legacy to her two daughters.

She mentioned that her mother had been 'spiritual' and that they had once sought help from a spiritualist years ago. I felt that this was the open door for me to minister more deeply to her unmet need of love and affirmation, and that she was spiritually open, a person of peace. I gave her a piece of my pottery with the word 'Courage' and began to affirm her. I told her that she was actually a courageous woman, an inspiration to her children, and the pride and joy of her heavenly Father. She allowed me to pray for her, and as I did so, I could feel the presence of the gentle, loving, affirming Holy Spirit touching those barren areas of her heart.

In praying together we committed her mother to Jesus, thanking him for her amazing life. I spoke words of the Father's affirmation, joy and delight in her as a person that he deeply loved. And then I released courage over her to live free of guilt, and to tell a different story with the rest of her life, than the one she had been contemplating.

After this prayer she looked up through her tears and seemed reflective, then she thanked me and we smiled at each other, knowing that God had set this meeting up as an intervention.

♡ ♡

God is a responder to those who are broken-hearted; he is not uninvolved in our suffering, and he is the one who is able to bind up broken hearts and comfort those who mourn.

In this setting, just to listen and be available in this context of bereavement, was going to be good in itself, but that brief connection to the perfect parent that God is to us, both father and mother, may have changed the course of this woman's destiny.

I am so thankful to him once again for his wisdom, kindness and perfect timing, and for leading me to be able to minister to a person's deepest felt needs. An urgent spiritual intervention, resulting in perhaps a year of the Lord's favour.

Chapter 15 – Dealing With Anger God's Way

A wonderfully honest, vulnerable and authentic lady happened to be on my list, to discuss her ongoing HRT. This was a simple consultation and easy to rejoice in a happy resolution for someone's physical symptoms. But all was not well with this lady and much was simmering underneath her pleasant persona during our phone consultation. She asked me if I knew of anyone to help her deal with her anger.

I had spent some time with her the previous autumn, listening to her story. In short, her father-in-law had made sexual advances towards her, on more than one occasion, when invited into her family home. The behaviour was inappropriate and deeply disturbing. When she told her husband, he went and confronted his father, who admitted his inappropriate behaviour. But instead of making restitution, the two men decided it was better for the family to cover it up and not risk upsetting his wife, my patient's mother-in-law. No one was to know about his misdemeanour; in time, it could be quietly forgotten.

Instead, what followed was increasing tension in the family. The woman felt silenced, bound never to speak of it at home or to the wider family. She felt coerced into allowing her father-in-law to continue to come into the family home as if nothing had happened, and reached a point where she felt her only option was to make excuses to be out of the house while he was there. After a period of time the marriage came under stress to the point that they agreed to separate. She left the home completely and now divorce seemed the only option left open to them.

Today, on this phone call, she told me more about her feelings of disturbing rage and anger, which had never been resolved and were making her feel physically unwell, and disrupting all her other relationships. All the usual channels for counselling which she had accessed had not been able to help her break free of her anger. She asked me about other options, and I said I would have a think about it. Then

I sensed the Holy Spirit prompting me, 'You know how to minister to people in this situation. You do it. Speak to her about forgiveness. I want to heal her heart.'

So I told her I had an idea of my own that might help her. It would be a bit radical, but if she was willing, I could see her that morning and we could see what might happen. She was ready to try anything and consented to come and see me later. It seemed to me that God had prepared the way. I had twenty minutes spare to prepare a plan for our time together, and because she was my last patient we had at least half an hour, which is very rare.

As she sat in the Mercy Seat and began to share her feelings, Holy Spirit was present to meet her there. I showed her a piece of art I have made, with black oil paint smudges, and red words written across it randomly: anger, hatred, rage, bitterness, disappointment, sadness, fear etc. I asked her which ones she related to the most, and she immediately pointed towards 'hatred' and 'rage', and her eyes began to fill with tears. Clearly these emotions had become enmeshed in her heart, affecting almost everything she did and all the people she loved and cared about. She was standing on the edge of something that felt like a black void and she was terrified.

Then I told her about something called the REFER tool, which my church often uses in church-based healing ministry. REFER is an acronym for a stepwise approach to dealing with anger and other negative emotions.

R stands for Realise: realise what is actually being felt and experienced.

E stands for Express: express all the emotion connected to the experience.

F stands for Forgive: forgive the person or people involved.

E stands for Eject: eject the lies believed as a result of the wounds experienced.

R stands for Replace: replace the lies with truths about who we truly are in God's eyes, our true identity.

I explained openly that this tool was developed in a church context to help people access emotional healing and I asked her permission to take her through it. She agreed, and with the wisdom and discernment of the Holy Spirit, I was able to help her identify specifically the wounds and the lies that she had come to believe: that she was less important than her in-laws; that she was unseen, unheard, dismissed and unimportant in the family; that her worth was less than everyone else's; that she was just an angry, bitter woman that no one really loved or wanted to be around; and that the only justice available to her was that which she created for herself by becoming an impenetrable fortress of anger. And finally, we identified the fear of a lonely future separated from her children and wider family.

The Father's love for people is so strong that he loves to tear down these horrible lies that crush a beautiful soul. We identified them for what they were, one by one, and after expressing her pain she was ready to talk about forgiveness. She understood that bitterness was like drinking poison and hoping the other person would die. She understood that people are flawed, and sometimes their responses are weak and fear-filled. And she understood about referring our injustice or offence to God and allowing him to take his rightful place as judge, while renouncing our own right to judge any more.

I asked her to visualise her father-in-law and husband in a boat, with her holding onto the mooring rope, representing her desperation to hold onto her anger as her protection. I asked her to imagine her heavenly Father right by her side, inviting her to trust him and let go of the rope, so that he could take on its burden. He was showing her that he was proud of her courage and her decision to come today, and that he wanted to show her his love, his honour of his daughter and restore her dignity.

As she quietly sat there with her tears in her eyes, I asked her how she was feeling. She replied, 'Really strange.'

I asked her, 'Do you feel safe?' and she said yes. I asked her, 'Do you feel heard and seen? Do you feel loved?' And she replied yes to each.

When I asked her if she could let go of the rope now, she said 'I'm not sure I'm ready yet, but I now believe I can do this, and I know how.' I gave her some notes to look at on her own or with a trusted friend, and put away my piece of art with all the toxic emotions written on it, saying, 'This is not for you anymore!'

We sat there for a moment to take stock of what had just happened, both very surprised and smiling at each other. The Holy Spirit was still very much present in the room. She hugged me and said, 'Thank you so much! And I only rang up about HRT!'

After she left, I was filled with awe once again at this divine set up. The day before, I had been reading testimonies from various sources on the internet about miracles experienced around the nations of the world. They all seemed to have arrived in my inbox in the same week – miracles of multiplication of food in a refugee centre on the Mexico/USA border; healing miracles, including that of a withered hand of a man in the USA; a dream in which Jesus appeared to a man in China, resulting in his whole family becoming Christians and his mother's depression being healed; the provision of coins and notes falling out of a pocket hanging over the rail in a tenement block in Uzbekistan, providing a poor single mother with enough money for the next week's food. Really, is there anything the Father can't or won't do? He is the master of originality, and loves to show up in a myriad of different ways. Whenever I am filled with the memory of these kinds of stories, I am able to access more faith to believe he is present and willing to show up for my work with patients. He does so every time, as long as I am obedient and sensitive to his promptings.

Another factor which I believe gave me the extra faith and courage for this was the fact that I had fasted and prayed twice in the week preceding, in order to seek God for more authority for getting breakthrough for people in otherwise impossible situations, physical and mental/emotional. We just need more of him in every way!

Chapter 16 – The Gift of a Frying Pan

'A gift opens the way and ushers the giver into the presence of
the great.'
Proverbs 18:16

'Blessed are the poor in spirit, for theirs is the kingdom of heaven.'
Matthew 5:3

One of the first people I ever saw the kingdom of heaven open up over,
with such ease and immediate effect, was a man called Denny. I want to
tell his story here because I recently saw him again after many years, and
the Holy Spirit reminded me of his grace working in and through this
dear man as the result of a gift. He asked me to allow his real name to be
shared in the telling of his story.

Denny was going through a really tough patch – you might describe
it as a mental and emotional breakdown. He was in his mid-forties and
struggling financially. He had lost his job, and was at breaking point
trying to navigate the process of applying for benefits, in order to pay
his rent, stay afloat, and stay in his home. The problem was made worse
by the fact that he was very limited in what he could read or write.
This came to light during one of our consultations when I gave him
something to read and he was forced to disclose that he couldn't read
it. The shame and embarrassment of this was adding to his desperation
and real financial plight. He was also estranged from his sons, who
lived with their mother, and his wider family was not forthcoming in
helping him.

He poured out his troubles one after the other, and finished by telling
me that someone in the area had broken into his house and stolen some
of his meagre possessions. To cap it all, he exclaimed, 'They even stole

my frying pan!' He was in tears. This was the final straw for him – that he had nothing to cook with!

I remember listening to him and my heart just welling up with compassion, I heard Holy Spirit speak to me. 'I want you to give him your frying pan and fill it with a bunch of fry-up foods – sausages, bacon, eggs, bread, etc.'

So I registered this in my mind, then proceeded to explain to him that he had a heavenly Father who loved him and was his provider and protector. I prayed for him and in doing so was able to release the affection of the Father over him in a tender moment of intimate connection. The Holy Spirit was suddenly manifestly present for this dear son who had lost just about everything and everyone. We chatted some more before he left with the plan we had agreed for the ongoing management of his mental health needs.

I went home for lunch and, galvanised by the instructions of the Holy Spirit, found him my frying pan, and popped into the local store for everything else I needed. Then I called him and asked him to come back to the surgery to collect something that I had for him. His eyes just popped out of his head with excitement when he saw the bag of goods, and I could sense his surprise and bewilderment all at the same time! So off he went and I didn't see him again for a month, when he came back for his follow-up review.

This time he sat down with intent and an earnest look on his face, and before I could even ask him how he was, he exclaimed, 'The frying pan! Oh man! Now I really understand that my heavenly Father loves me and will take care of me! What you said to me, it all fell into place!'

God had revealed this timeless and most important of all revelations to this one illiterate man in a heartbeat, all because of a gift and some words in his time of need. From that time on we have had a wonderful doctor-patient relationship, and it opened my heart again to see the Father's desire to meet with people on a whole new level.

I did not see Denny again for a few years but last week he needed to come in for some physical symptoms, and for an asthma check-up.

Interestingly, before I left for work on the very morning that Denny rang, I felt I needed my husband to pray for me and asked him to pray whatever was on his heart, whatever the Holy Spirit showed him, because in myself I felt rather flat, tired and low on expectation. Steve prayed that I would see people as the Father saw them, have the mind of Jesus about them, and speak the Father's words of affirmation over them. I knew then that I was to stop for someone...

So in he came, both of us a little more grey-haired than before! This time he told me that he was in a good place now. He was working again, had been reconciled with his two sons, and was feeling really stable emotionally, and enjoying his life. There were some pain issues that were hindering him from being able to do his job, but that was all.

After we finished the medical part of his consultation, I asked him if I could pray for him. He was thrilled and immediately bowed his head and took my hands, sitting in the same Mercy Seat where he first encountered the Father's love. I was able to tell him that the Father was really looking forward this day to speaking his words of encouragement over him, and had prepared me beforehand with what he wanted to say. Then I spoke a simple prophetic message over him, expressing the Father's pleasure and pride in him, saying how I sensed the Father's pleasure and pride in him, and I prayed for physical healing from pain and asthma.

On a final note, when I knocked on his door on Christmas Eve, laden with some Christmas cake, to ask him for his permission for his story to be told, he gladly invited me in to his and his sons nicely decorated 'man cave! I was amazed at the transformation, and was so glad to be able to see him in his own home, settled, secure in his identity and extremely happy. His son was out at work and I could sense he was very proud of him. He was thrilled about the story being told, and keen for others to be helped as he had once been .

I love this story, and the timely follow-up. It again makes me realise how much the Holy Spirit wants to connect with people, and how there are some people who are just ripe for his love and the message of adoption. I marvel at how a simple but radical gift can open the door for so much more. I wonder how many more conversations about deep, profound yet simple spiritual truths could be had, by simply being generous and opening the way for the presence of Jesus, so that he can do what we could never do on our own, no matter how well-intentioned.

And I wonder at the truth Jesus taught: 'Blessed are the poor in spirit, for theirs is the kingdom of heaven.'

Chapter 17 – Love Looks Like Something

There is something the Father always wants to communicate to every individual, and that is that he dearly loves them. What love may actually look like to that person is different in each situation, but if we are ready and willing, the Holy Spirit will show us what to do.

He sat in the chair, after a painful, laboured walk from the waiting room. His legs were swollen and his clothes ragged and unwashed. The odour of poverty and neglect filled the room. His beard was untidy, and his face covered in psoriasis. His hands were rough, and his fingers and thumb were wrapped in a dirty bandage in an attempt to cover burn wounds. His shirt was too small for him and the buttons in the mid-section had long fallen off. All this I took in as I looked at him sitting there. I tried to fix my attention on his face, but found all I could focus on was his feet, stuffed into some old trainers, the laces long gone, and clearly swollen and dirt-encrusted.

This dear man's body had a long and painful story to tell. A former heroin addict, he had multiple thromboses in his legs, impairing his venous drainage. Loss of sensation in his hands and feet was due to a nerve damage disorder linked to diabetes, which was the end result of years of neglect, poor diet, weight gain and antipsychotic medication. In addition, he had a stooping posture due to osteoarthritis in his back and a limp due to hip arthritis. In addition to all these physical conditions, he suffered from mental illness including past psychosis, depression and almost total loss of executive function. He was broken, inside and out.

But the thing about him is that he was a believer, born again many years ago, and amazingly delivered from addiction to heroin. He had been doing well for some years, seeking to be a peer mentor with Aspire, our local drug treatment centre, and he had friends. But life in his damaged body was becoming harder and harder for him to manage, the decline slow and unrelenting. He remained full of faith, however, and I always felt he had a connection to the Father's heart. We always prayed together for healing of heart, body and soul. He felt marginalised when it came to church, and the one couple who faithfully ministered to him and looked after his practical needs for many years, were no longer available due to their own personal tragedies.

His mother lived in Glasgow, which is where he was originally from, and every few months he travelled up there by train to spend a month with her. These trips were his time to reboot as she totally spoilt him and took care of him, shaving him, applying the creams and ointments, feeding him home-cooked food, giving him a haircut and washing his clothes. He told me he was about to go to Glasgow the next weekend, and I wondered how his mother would feel, seeing him like this once again.

I asked him, 'What shoe size are you?' and he said, 'Ten.' I thought to myself, 'OK, I am going to get him some new trainers, and some shirts to travel up to Scotland in, some nice colourful shirts.' As I went to buy them, I imagined those feet sporting clean, new socks and shoes, and even what it would look like to wash those feet! Then I took them to his home. When I arrived, he opened the door and I presented him with his gifts. His face lit up with happiness and we began to talk about his upcoming trip. I spoke some words of life, healing and destiny over him. We prayed, and then he literally leaned his head on my shoulder and I hugged him. Neighbours were at their doorsteps watching; evidently he was well known, notorious, no doubt, because of his self-neglect.

I felt we were in a moment in time when heaven had just invaded earth, and delivered some loving kindness, provision and honour to a person the world would consider the least of society.

He has continued to suffer with all these conditions, although he is much more stable and settled than he once was. Sadly, when I connected with him recently, he told me that his mother in Glasgow had now succumbed to pneumonia and died, leaving him and his brother (who also suffers from major mental illness) as orphans. He was unable to connect to his emotions and cry his tears of grief, because his brain is so affected by all the drugs he needs to take to suppress the voices he hears. But he let me pray for him and tenderly minister to his grief, as well as celebrate his amazing, faithful mother, who remained on duty for her sons until her eighty-fourth year of life.

When I think about this dear man with a heart of gold and a strong faith in Jesus, I feel he may be just too broken in this life, and it weighs heavily on me sometimes, that I can't do more to help him. Many people have stopped for him over the years and tried to help, and it's no one's fault that he can't be 'fixed.' But I know that I can show him what love looks like each time I see him, and that he knows the heart of the Father for him, and that one day he will be compensated. Jesus will switch his old ruined body for a glorious one, and he will be everything the Father originally designed him to be. In the meantime, I will always stop for him, and give him in every way I can a sense of his worth and value and dignity. He is, and always will be, worthy to be loved.

Healing in the Workplace

The following are things that I have learned on my journey with Holy Spirit, and may be helpful for you as you have read this book and are beginning to think about how you could see the above worked out in your lives.

1. My room is not just a place to complete my tasks, but a place for encounter. It's a place for me to encounter God myself, to be changed, to learn and grow in understanding and humility, to be moved with compassion, and to handle disappointment with grace and patience. I set it up that way with prophetic art on the walls, postcards over my desk describing kingdom values, a plug-in diffuser giving off a pleasant fragrance, and I pray for the presence of the Holy Spirit to fill the room when I work there. My desk is like an altar, where I will lay down my life for patients and for my colleagues. The patient's chair becomes a 'mercy seat' and no matter what happens, they will leave there feeling better than when they walked in. I 'check my heart' at the door and make sure I'm not carrying in an atmosphere of anxiety, anger or resentment. If I sense any of those things I pray and bring them to the Father , give them to him, and ask him to release his truth, his love and the reality of his kingdom presence in the place of those emotions.

2. The preparation begins in the secret place of prayer and fellowship with Jesus and binding of my heart to his and to Scripture. There are some special ones that I read repeatedly and which always help me access faith and compassion for people.

'The spirit of the Sovereign Lord is upon me, because the Lord has anointed me to proclaim good news to the poor. He has sent me to bind up the broken-hearted, to proclaim freedom for the captives, to proclaim the year of the Lord's favour... to comfort all who mourn, and provide for those who grieve in Zion – to bestow on them a crown of beauty instead of ashes, the oil of joy instead of mourning... ' Isaiah 61:1-3

'The Sovereign Lord has given me a well-instructed tongue, to know the word that sustains the weary. He wakens me morning by morning, wakens my ear to listen like one being instructed.' Isaiah 50:3-4

'Comfort, comfort my people,' says your God. Speak tenderly to Jerusalem and proclaim to her that her hard service has been completed...' Isaiah 40:1-2

'Arise, shine, for your light has come, and the glory of the Lord rises upon you. See darkness covers the earth, thick darkness is over the peoples, but the LORD rises upon you and his glory appears over you.' Isaiah 60:1-2

What happens in my prayer life is the foundation of all risk and faith that results later in action. If I haven't first visualised something and thought it through on my own with Jesus, and felt his pleasure in it, I simply won't attempt it. If I am feeling depleted and in need of time alone with God, I will take that time and prioritise it before I can sense faith arising in me again. It is good to recognise when we are depleted, and make sure we come back into his presence for refuelling. We need to pay attention to our Holy Spirit fuel gauge and see if we have enough in the tank!

3. We must cultivate expectation for the miraculous. Healing is in the kingdom, and the kingdom is at hand. We need to believe God is healing today and that he wants to work with us! During a busy day, I am looking, listening, and trying to remind myself of any testimony I have heard. It is important not to become immune to the wonder of those stories, but to hold on to the wonder and rise of faith that we felt when we first heard them.

I sometimes play a worship song, 'May I never lose the wonder...wide eyed and mystified, may I be just like a child, staring at the beauty of the king.' Every day something new and wonderful will happen, if we expect him to show up! When I've seen something God is doing or has done, I take a moment to thank him. I worship him, celebrate everything that goes well, and sometimes record my own stories and testimonies so that I don't forget them.

4. Be aware of what we carry within us. We all have access to the heavenly realms, where there is an abundant supply of every spiritual blessing available to us, as well as his delegated authority to release it on others. I sometimes think of myself as carrying my spiritual medical bag with all the kingdom attributes and resources inside. I ask the Lord, 'What is most needed in this situation? Which one shall I release upon this person? Is it peace they need? Is it love? Freedom?' etc. I have heard it said that love, peace and joy are members of one family; just try and get one into the situation, and the others will follow.

5. Recognising his presence as an utmost priority. We simply can't afford to get into human striving on our own – we will just run into closed doors!

Out of a possible ten doors, nine may well be closed, due to the pressures of political correctness, a spirit of offence, fear, traditions, or resistance of the demonic. But if we try gently pushing open the tenth door, the place where we invite his presence and see what he wants to do, it is going to open. It's about finding the 'soft place'. Imagine his presence finding its way under the threshold of a locked door, or through the keyhole. There are no barriers when he shows up, and anything can happen.

6. Move heaven's resources through creative expression to meet human need. I have developed many ways of communicating the Father's heart to people, sometimes in the language of psychology, relaying knowledge and understanding to them about their condition, sometimes overtly spiritual. I take them on a journey, and they can go along as far as they want to. People are allowed to be ministered to spiritually according to the NICE guidelines, as long as they are asked for their permission and are willing for that to happen. We may ask ourselves, "What does this person need?" We may ask the person directly, "What do you feel you most need right now?" How we convey what the Father wants to say or do for this person may involve using inspired creativity, the prophetic in its various forms such as pictures, songs, words of wisdom, scriptures, or charts and diagrams describing their chosen path until now and the better path towards healing and wholeness. It doesn't really matter, what matters is that the person can connect with what the Father wants them to know, and take a step towards his intended life of freedom for them.

7. Remember that healing looks like many things. It may be that the person needs medicine, or a good check-up, or a surgical procedure. Maybe it will look like you praying for them and something like a supernatural miracle that is either sudden and unexpected, or gradually evident over time. Sometimes people need to learn to take responsibility for themselves, to make lifestyle changes, brave decisions, better choices. Sometimes it is about learning to see themselves as God sees them. All of these things may help to allow natural healing to take place. Our bodies carry the amazing ability to heal naturally, which is a miracle in itself.

8. Most important of all for me is friendship with The Holy Spirit. Learning how to know his voice clearly is an exciting journey and a wonderful adventure, one that needs and deserves lots of practice.

Learning to be aware of what he is wanting to do involves stopping to listen, or asking him direct questions. Remember the tone of his voice is not, 'I need you to be courageous and take risks and share my heart with people today, otherwise those people will perish, because you're their only hope.' That just causes undue pressure, guilt, and forced, unnatural actions which can lead to the person feeling really uncomfortable or thinking that we are weird!

His voice sounds more like this: 'Today I'm going to be healing, loving, encouraging, saving, delivering people, and I'd love you to partner with me in this work. Are you up for that?'

That's the reversal of responsibility, and much more of a shared partnership. We can look on it as an adventurous internship or apprenticeship. I get to learn, grow and celebrate what goes well, as well as make mistakes and miss the mark some of the time – and it's all OK!

Proverbs 13:17 says, 'A trustworthy envoy brings HEALING.' (emphasis mine)

Never was there a time in history where healing is more needed and relevant to everyone's lives, including our own. And we are trustworthy envoys of the kingdom of heaven. Healing is in the kingdom, as are justice, peace, deliverance, provision, and joy. I love this definition of an envoy from the Oxford English Dictionary:

'An envoy is a representative of a government, who is sent on a special diplomatic mission'

I am a trained healthcare professional, but this statement implies that kingdom healing is for all of us as believers sent on a diplomatic mission to people we meet in our sphere of work and influence.

The whole earth (not just the whole church!) shall be filled with the knowledge of the glory of the Lord, and this must include our places of work.

In my job, the goal is to help get people well and whole. So I must address their biology and physiology, their emotional wellbeing, their spirit and their identity. I refuse to polarise healing experiences into 'medical' or 'spiritual'. People are triune beings, and need integration of body, soul and spirit. They need understanding of their eternal value, their significance, complexity and individual beauty. I want to pursue all kinds of journeys that equip me better to help people become well, healthy and whole. I know no one better than the Holy Spirit to teach me both how and when to minister sensitively and effectively to the whole person. He is my perfect counsellor, the Prince of Peace, the everlasting Father and Almighty God.

Sustainability

Being on the receiving end of so many sad stories and engaging with people in their time of need can be exhausting. I am no different from any of my healthcare professional colleagues, who daily show up and avail themselves of people's need to tell their stories, and then respond to them with everything they know to do, using everything they have learned, everything they have in their bag of experience, and all the energy they have within them. It can feel like weathering, a kind of wearing down. Eventually, if we aren't careful, we get compassion fatigue, and can no longer engage like we used to. We begin to wither.

I have learned so much about rest, the need for a rhythm of life that includes rest, restoration, fun, friendship and solitude. God wants us to prosper in our body, soul and spirit. Life can't be all about ministry and work.

I have just returned from a holiday in Wales with Steve my husband and our dog Finney. There we enjoyed the riches of nature: solitude, the wonder of creation in the form of waterfalls, ravines, forests and rolling green hills, sheep and all kinds of beautiful birds and wildlife coming to our cabin, and discovering adventure in unplanned trips, spontaneity, laughter, banter, giant Toblerone chocolate, and lots of sport on TV!

God spoke to me one day through an amazing cascade of waterfalls where a torrent came crashing down into a large, clear pool. This then overflowed over the front of the rock face into another smaller waterfall, which fell into another pool, and so on at several more levels until it came to settle into a stream flowing out of the valley below. As I stopped, mesmerised by all this, and listening to the noise of the rushing waters, I knew that it was a picture God wanted me to see about my life – to be that pool, receiving the river of the Holy Spirit, waiting to be filled to the brim, before overflowing and resourcing others, who would do the exact same thing in their turn. Water always falls to the lowest place, so just being postured to kneel and wait upon the Lord, resting in him, not trying in my own strength, seems the best way to remain full to the brim.

There are some things that are just true, no matter which way you look at life. The hard facts are that there are too many needs, and too much sadness in the world. There are people that just I can't help. There are days that don't go especially well. There are diseases that ruin and destroy people's lives no matter what medicine we give, and what treatments we plan. People get older and bodies are fragile. I'm getting older and I feel fragile at times! And sometimes I just don't feel like going into work!

But there are also higher truths, and this is where we need to focus intentionally as often as we can. It is as simple as looking at his face and being reminded that God is a master of the impossible. He is the Lord of adventure. He can provide solutions for any problem. He will always come when invited. He is willing to partner with us in our work. He is kind and loving and his presence in the room makes all the difference to an outcome. He is the God of hope. He is the personification of joy. He is the Prince of Peace. He is the redeemer of tragedies. He never tires or grows weary. He lives in me and you!

Final note

I hope that this collection of stories has been helpful in some way, and I pray that as your adventure goes on and on through everyday life, you continue to discover just how merciful and beautiful the heart of God really is. It never diminishes; He never grows weary or fatigued. There is always more, and no matter how difficult this current season in the nations may seem to be as we listen to the news stories, remember it's our time to rise and shine! The glory of the Lord really is upon us, and his wings of mercy are over us as we reach out to the one in front of us.

One of my favourite prayers is Paul's prayer in Philippians 1:9-11:

'And this is my prayer: that your love may abound more and more in knowledge and depth of insight, so that you may be able to discern what is best and may be pure and blameless for the day of Christ, filled with the fruit of righteousness that comes through Jesus Christ – to the glory and praise of God.'

So I pray for you, as you read this book:

May your love abound more and more as you approach your place of work, and may you gain more understanding of God's heart of mercy, and be filled with all kinds of inspired creative ideas to help people connect with his heart. May you be rooted in the wisdom, discernment and guidance of the Holy Spirit, may your work place become a fruitful place of healing and restoration, and may you be incredibly blessed and filled with joy as you partner with God in all of this!